A TREASURY OF WINNING BASKETBALL TIPS

A TREASURY OF WINNING BASKETBALL TIPS

BOB SAMARAS

PARKER PUBLISHING COMPANY, INC.
WEST NYACK, NY

Library of Congress Cataloging in Publication Data
Samaras, Bob
  A treasury of winning basketball tips.
  Includes index.
    1. Basketball—Coaching. I. Title.
GV885.3.S25 1984   796.32'3077   83-22104

ISBN 0-13-930199-2

To my lovely wife, Marietta, and my daughters Debbie, Nikki, and Valeri for their love, affection, encouragement, and support, while making it possible for me to enjoy coaching the wonderful game of basketball.

ACKNOWLEDGMENTS

To Dr. Leon A. Lande, retired Professor of Health and Physical Education and former coach at Wayne State University for an excellent job of proofreading, reviewing, and editing the manuscript.

To all of the players, both young and old, whom I had the privilege to coach throughout the years.

To my former assistant and close personal friend, George Petrouleas, and to former assistants Cal Dilworth and Ed Jones for their encouragement and support.

To the many coaches on all levels of basketball in the United States, Canada, and Greece with whom I have had the privilege to associate through the years, especially to Lou Carnecessa and Jack Kaiser of St. John's University, Bob Zuffelato and Jim Kelly, formerly of Marshall University, and to the late Stu Aberdeen of Marshall University, who gave so much to the game of basketball and who was a close personal friend.

To all of my personal friends too numerous to mention here who have supported and contributed to our basketball programs throughout the years.

To Herman L. Masin, Editor, **Scholastic Coach Magazine**, for his permission to use "The Automatic Twenty-Second Offense"; also for his help and encouragement in writing for publication.

To Addamae Akin, Counselor, Roseville High School, Roseville, Michigan, for making arrangements, and to typing teacher Joyce W. Swartout and the Vocational Stenographic Class, for typing out the first copy of the manuscript.

WHY THIS BOOK
IS VALUABLE TO YOU

If you are like most coaches, you are constantly searching for ideas to improve your basketball program, especially since winning programs reflect continual upgrading and improvement. Most coaches spend hours seeking ideas to help refine the playing system through correcting faults, revising, and adding new twists to some maneuvers. Time is also spent learning more about players' personalities, about player-coach communication, and how to motivate players. Additional time is often allotted to improving game planning and individual player and game evaluation. The effort to seek perfection is a continuous, ongoing process and very time-consuming.

This book contains forty proven winning tips, which offer a wealth of material to help you improve your program. These tips have been used and tested in winning basketball programs at all levels of competition. Each tip can easily be incorporated into any system of play.

Here are practical tips in the critical areas of Defense, Transition Game, Offense, Special Situations, Practice, Psychology and Evaluation. The form for each tip in the first five areas includes three parts. The **Overview** is the first, which serves to explain the background and reason for using the tip. The second is the **Execution**, which is the explanation and diagramming of the play, and the third is **Coaching Points**, which explains how to utilize the tip most effectively. The Psychology and Evaluation tips are presented in general text form.

There is something for every coach in this versatile conglomeration of ideas. There are ideas to help when you wish to make a simple adjustment in one phase of your playing system as well as to a complete, independent offense. An example of the former is Tip 2, "Adding Combination Principles to Zone or Man-to-Man Defense." An example of the latter is Tip 18, "Using the Figure Eight Offense to Attack Zone and Combination Defenses."

Going beyond the playing system, there are occasions when you will seek ideas to streamline team practices, to avoid wasting time, or to find a better motivation system. This treasury contains tips for all of these problems.

You will find that different problems arise during various segments of the basketball season. There are many answers available for these problems, too. For example, if your team is having difficulty scoring in the last minute of close games late in the season, you should refer to the tip on "Special Plays for Last-Second Scoring."

These tips can be used regardless of your philosophy of play, or the skill level, size, or speed of your players. There are tips available to help a struggling team seeking to improve, or a team zeroing in on a championship. The tips are based on fundamentally sound basketball principles.

Another reason this book can be valuable evolves around the creativeness of the coach. I have always contended that coaches tend to be ingenious and relatively creative. These tips can serve as a stimulus to a coach who will take the idea and add his own innovation to make it even more useful. The true value of an idea is to set the foundation for new and better ideas to emerge.

Finally, if you take advantage of these tips, your basketball program should be strengthened. The formulation of new strategies, tactics, and maneuvers should increase your team's winning potential. After all, the bottom line in any basketball program is still winning more games. You will find yourself keeping this Treasury of Tips in a handy spot on your desk available for continual reference.

Note: I have used the masculine gender when referring to coaches and players. This was done to avoid the awkward "he or she" and similar expressions. I am well aware that a significant number of coaches and players are women, and this book speaks every bit as much to them as to their male counterparts.

Bob Samaras

CONTENTS

SYMBOLS USED IN DIAGRAMS

① ② ③ ④ ⑤   **Offensive Players**

①   **Player with Ball**

X1 X2 X3 X4 X5   **Defensive Players**

〜〜〜〜〜〜〜→   **Dribble**

– – – –1– – – →   **Pass (Small number indicates number of pass in that sequence).**

———2———→   **Movement of player (Small number indicates number of player movement in that sequence).**

    Jab Step

———————⊣   **Screen**

———————⇃   **Screen and Roll**

————〜〜→   **Change of Pace**

———————⊣   **Defensive Pinch (or trap)**

⊠   **Coach**

TIP 1

Changing Defenses
Systematically

OVERVIEW

A basketball team should be built around a versatile playing system, which should encompass multiple offenses and defenses. To win consistently, a team must change offenses and defenses often. It is difficult to count on a particular offense or defense for the entire season, especially when you consider the various types of play situations available to the opposition.

The focus of this tip is the defensive system. There are two things to consider when using a multiple-defense attack. The first is the development of several team defenses, and the second is the establishment of coach-player communication systems to change from one defense to another.

The selection of multiple defenses must include full-court presses, half-court presses, and drop-back (quarter-court) defenses. There should be a minimum of two defenses for each type of zone and man-to-man defenses. Other options should be added to make a defense more effective. For example, the **Funnel** and **Fan** options might be integrated into the drop-back man-for-man defense, with the primary thrust being to influence the ball movement toward the center (Funnel) or to the sidelines (Fan). Trapping in the baseline-sideline corners could be an option added to either the drop-back man-to-man or any drop-back zone. There are other complicated options that can be added or designed to develop a stronger defense, but the multiple defenses in this tip are the basic types.

There are three ways to change a defense during a game. One is by calling time-out, permitting you to confer with the players on the change. Another is during a delay in the action such as free-throw shooting, out-of-bounds plays, and jump-ball plays. The third is during a slowdown in various game situations. The methods of communication will be discussed in detail later in the tip.

The defenses to be used can be discussed in the game plan, but generally all of the team's basic defenses could be initiated at any time during the game, because an opponent might use tactics that would need a counter move not accounted for in the basic game plan. Flexibility is the key—the basic defenses should be available at any time. Multiple-type defenses are designed with the following eight objectives in mind:

1. To confuse the opponent
2. To continually force adjustments by the opponent
3. To take charge of tempo
4. To stop the opponent's momentum
5. To probe for weaknesses of the opponent's personnel
6. To keep the opponent off balance
7. To determine which defense is most effective
8. To upset the opponent psychologically.

EXECUTION

When developing a group of defenses as a style of play, select those that are the most basic, and then develop others according to demands. In the earlier part of the basketball season, the less complicated options should be taught. For example, when using full-court presses, if the defense is man-for-man, then the drop-back defense should automatically be the same. When necessary, a change of defense may take place by brief communication with the coach. We have found that eight basic defenses work most effectively in our multiple-defenses scheme. They are the:

1. Full-court man-for-man press
2. Full-court 2-2-1 zone press
3. Full-court Diamond (1-2-1-1) zone press
4. Half-court man-for-man press
5. Diamond half-court zone press
6. Drop-back man-for-man

7. Drop back 2-1-2 zone
8. Drop back 1-3-1 zone.

A general rule of thumb is to start the first two minutes of the game and second half with the full-court man-for-man press. This gives the player time to establish man-to-man responsibility prior to shifting to zone-type defenses. Along the same line, each player should always be conscious of a tentative man-to-man assignment. Even when the switch to a zone defense takes place, players should develop a defensive rhythm.

When the man-for-man press is used to begin the game and during the second half, defensive changes can be made with less difficulty. The following three types of changes may take place: (1) changes within the man-to-man group, (2) changes to and within the zone group, and (3) a combination of both, for example, a full-court man-to-man press with a zone drop-back defense. The man-to-man type of defense is the basic defense from which all the other defenses have been contrived.

Number Signals

The next logical step is to establish a set of signals that will permit the changing of defenses to take place smoothly. There are several different types of signals for communicating.

Your goal is to make changes during the game in progress, without calling a time-out. Probably the easiest method to accomplish this is to give each defense the number listed under the basic defenses. The coach can indicate either verbally or by hand signals the defense desired. The player receiving the signals indicates by word of mouth or by holding up the proper number of fingers to his teammates. A team huddle at the free throw line just prior to a free throw attempt is an excellent time to relay the message. If a player misses the signal, another signal can be given by the player not informed. A teammate can then repeat the number verbally or by a display of hand signals.

Automatic Signals

Another set of signals can originate automatically from the player movements or from opposing player movements or alignments. For example, if the team is in a basic drop back 2-1-2 zone and the opposition sets up in a one guard offensive alignment, the defense should shift to a 1-3-1 zone when a front defensive player attacks the point guard. Another example: a designated player moves from a drop-back zone front position to a point position at midcourt, which indicates that the Diamond half-court press is to be used. This generally takes place when the ball is slowly moving up-court. A change of position on defensive rebounding during a free throw attempt would indicate a Full-court diamond press. In high school games, the time left in a quarter during a foul shot attempt might indicate the defense. For example, three minutes and ten seconds might indicate that the number three defense (2-2-1 full court zone press) should be initiated.

Miscellaneous Signals

Another set of signals that could be used involve movements of the arms and hands. It is possible to initiate a variety of signals. For example, crossing arms or by holding the hands up or down could indicate other signals. Names of schools, professional teams or opponents may also be used as signals. Occasionally defenses may be changed by the quarter or by time blocks of four or eight minutes in a college game. Another method is changing after baskets or free throw attempts.

A final change could be made on the type of first pass of the offense pattern by the player dribbling the ball. A bounce pass could switch a basic drop-back defense from a zone to a man-for-man, or vice versa. All of these have been tried and proven successful by our teams at one time or other.

Changing defenses also has other advantages. The players enjoy the tactics, and find it amusing, especially when it confuses the opposition. This in turn gives the players more confidence.

COACHING POINTS

1. Develop a set of signals and practice them in drills and practice scrimmages.
2. If several substitutes enter a game in a short period of time, use the full-court man-for-man defense for at least two minutes.
3. Defense changing is most effective when the players attack the opponent aggressively.

4. Make note of the defenses that are the most effective and those that are the least effective.

5. Use a full-court press, a half-court press and a zone and man-to-man drop-back defense the first half to probe for opponent's personnel and pattern play weaknesses.

6. Use a "Help" signal by a player whenever there is a full-court defense break down, which is an automatic retreat to the three-second area defense.

7. Use a 2-1-2 zone for the three second area retreat defense. Have one player stop the forward progress of the ball as the retreat is being set up.

8. Have the players help develop various communication signals and methods.

TIP 2

Adding Combination Principles To Zone and Man-to-Man Defenses

OVERVIEW

The three categories of basketball defenses are: (1) the man-to-man, which emphasizes individual guarding responsibility of the **man** first, and then the area; (2) the zone, which involves the concept of following the ball first, and then guarding the man in an area; and (3) the combinations, which are a mixture of both types of defenses but **are basically more zone than man.**

It is important to employ at least the man-for-man and zone defenses. The combination defenses can be very complicated and therefore time-consuming to teach. A coach usually has a strong preference to teach a basic man-to-man or zone defense. It is a good policy to use and develop both types of defenses to a comparable degree so that the most effective defense is available in the proper game situation.

The man-to-man or the zones become much better defenses when coaches incorporate some tactics from each. This type of defense is considered a basic man-to-man or a zone with combination principles, and not really a combination defense. Both defenses will become stronger when the best principles of each are incorporated into the maneuvers, because if both are equally efficient, you may then select the one that best suits your needs during a game.

EXECUTION

The use of combination maneuvers in both defenses must have a zone foundation. This is accomplished by dividing the floor into four basic ball position areas. These four areas are shown in Diagram 2-1 and lettered A through D.

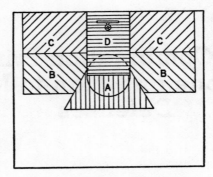

Diagram 2-1

The (A) area is cone-shaped and lies between the free throw line and three feet beyond the top of the circle; it extends five feet on each side of that circle at the top of the circle and one foot at the free throw line extended. The (B) area is located on both sides of the court just outside the three-second lane, five feet above and six feet below the free throw line extended to six feet from the sidelines. The (C) areas are the baseline on either side of the three-second lane up to six feet below the free throw line extended, to three feet from the sidelines. The (D) area is the three-second lane and post areas.

Area Ball Position Rules

An important point is that, in the zone defenses, the player alignments in relation to the ball position areas may vary with the ball in the (A) area, but the defensive alignments are constant with the ball in other areas. To explain further, with the ball in the (A) area, the defensive alignment can change from a one-guard to a two-guard front relative to the zone being implemented (for example, a 2-1-2, 3-2, 1-3-1 zone).

However, when the ball is in the (B) area, the player alignment is always a 1-3-1. When in a corner, or (C) area, the Flattened-out 2-3 alignment takes place. With the ball in the post areas, the 2-3 Convergence alignment is used. The B, C, and D defensive player alignments automatically take place as the players shift to follow the ball.

Diagrams 2-2, 2-3, 2-4 depict the zone alignments with the ball in the B, C, and D ball position areas. In Diagram 2-2 with the ball on the right free throw line extended area (B zone), the zone alignment becomes a 1-3-1 regardless of the zone being utilized. The middle man, X1, must always stay between the ball and the basket. The other players will usually stay within twenty feet of X1. Following the diagram, point-man X2 guards the ball handler O1, X3 is the defensive top wing man, X5 is the baseline wing man, X4 is the swing-man close to the basket on the left side of the court.

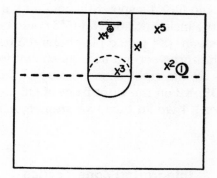

Diagram 2-2

Diagram 2-3 shows the ball in the corner. The zone becomes a Flattened-out 2-3. Player X5 is on the ball handler O1, X1 (defensive post-man) is between the ball and the basket. X1 should front a low post-man within eight feet of the basket. If the ball is beyond eight feet, X1 may play either in front or behind a post-man, depending on the post-man's abilities. X4 is behind X1 under the basket, while X2 and X3 play the top part of the zone.

The 2-3 Convergence alignment is used when the ball is in Area D, the post area. In Diagram 2-4, X1 stays between the post-man, ball handler O5, and the basket, while X1's teammates converge on O5. It is up to X1 to quickly maneuver behind the post-man if X1 was fronting the post-man.

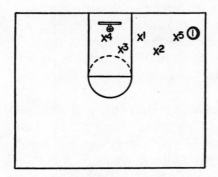

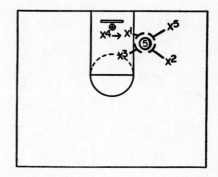

Diagram 2-3   **Diagram 2-4**

The following maneuver could take place if X1 is caught flat-footed while fronting the post-man. Player X4 could take the inside position and X1 could fill X4's spot. Still another shift could be made with X4 securing the inside position and X3 could take X4's area. X2 would fill X3's position. (X1 would play behind a post-man standing three feet from the three-second area as shown in Diagram 2-4.)

Player X5 is on the right baseline side of O5, X1 on the left baseline side of O5, X2 on the right front of O5, and X3 on the left front of O5. Player X4 would take two steps toward O5, then hold that position.

Integrating Zone Tactics
Into the Man-to-Man Defense

The two vital rules which are the back-bone for guarding offensive players individually in any man-to-man defense are: (1) the "Ball-You-Basket," and (2) the "Ball-You-Man." The first rule indicates the player guarding the ball handler must stay between him and the basket. The second rule means a player off-the-ball stays between his man and the ball. These two simple but vital rules are also conveniently adaptable in all zone defenses. (Both rules can be noted in Diagrams 2-5, 2-6, 2-7, and 2-8.)

In the man-to-man defense with the ball in the A area, the players play man-for-man with switching of men taking place as needed. The players off-the-ball can sag towards the basket. Permitting the ball in this area in the top position is undesirable defensively because the ball can be passed in six directions, to any side of the court, as shown in Diagram 2-5. Defensive players also have more court to cover. The concept then is to force the ball to either side of the court (Diagram 2-6). With the ball on a wing, it is more difficult for the offensive team to go to the basket. There are only five directions for a ball to be passed (two of them away from the basket). Also, the action takes place on one side of the court. Notice with the ball in the B area, 1-3-1 zone alignment is in effect. Player X2 guards the ball handler, O1; X1 plays between the ball and the basket (fronting his player, who is at a low-post position), X3 guards O2, and X4 guards O3, and X5 guarding O4 completes the 1-3-1 alignment.

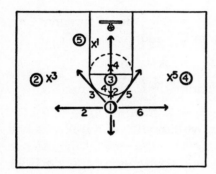

Diagram 2-5

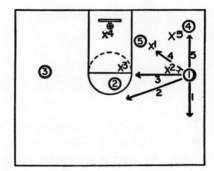

Diagram 2-6

In Diagram 2-7, the ball has been passed to the corner in the C area. The Flattened-out 2-3 zone alignment is in effect. Player X5 guards the player with the ball, O4; X1 fronts O5; X4 is under the basket; X2 plays a top position, and X3 is behind him, also on top.

When the ball goes into a post-man, then the D area defensive Convergence alignment is in effect as shown in Diagram 2-8. Player O5 has the ball in the post position; center-man X1 moves to play between him and the basket. (Either of the other two shifts could take place.) Players X2, X3, and X5 all converge on O5 in the D area to combat a shot attempt or a pass to another player. Meanwhile, X4 moves in front of the basket to watch for cutters.

These man-to-man shifts into zone alignments make it possible to guard the ball handler and receive both strongside and weakside help. Even if the offense is very mobile, the position of the ball triggers the zone tactics. Each defensive player using the two man-to-man rules must be conscious of the ball location, the zone align-

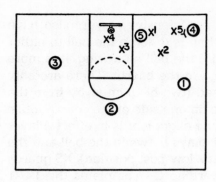

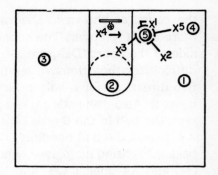

Diagram 2-7   **Diagram 2-8**

ment in effect, his position location within the alignment, plus switching man assignments to stay in the alignment.

Integrating Man-to-Man Tactics Into the Zones

The initial zone defensive alignment with the ball in the A area ball position is automatically a match-up zone triggered by the offense used. A point guard offense with a high post-man, triggers a 1-3-1 zone. A one-guard front without a post-man is matched up with a 3-2 zone. A two-guard offense dictates a 2-1-2 zone. Of course, the ball movement into the other areas automatically dictates the other three alignments. The important responsibility of each player is to shift quickly in his zone area following ball movement, then to play man-to-man defense with the "Ball-You-Basket" and "Ball-You-Man" rules on the offensive player in his zone.

Diagrams 2-9 and 2-10 depict two situations where man-to-man rules are integrated into the zone defense. In Diagram 2-9, wing man O1 passes the ball to O4, then cuts to the basket. X2 guards the cutter, discouraging a return pass, then X2 protects the low-post area temporarily until X1 or X4 signal verbally that player O1 is covered. At this time, X2 returns to look for another offensive player in the original zone. If X5 moved to cover a player in X2's zone, then X2 would fill in to X5's zone.

In Diagram 2-10, the theme is to control a dribbler. Offensive player O1 dribbles towards the basket with X2 forcing O1 to the baseline near the corner. Player X5 quickly fills X2's zone and X2 stays in X5's zone. The other players fill the C zone areas and use

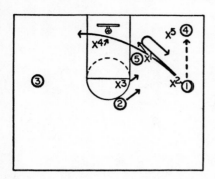

Diagram 2-9

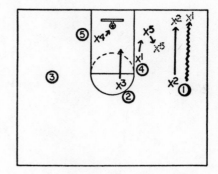

Diagram 2-10

the man-to-man rules to guard players in their zones. Communication between players is important and always necessary, particularly when players are switching zones.

COACHING POINTS

1. Force the ball movement toward the sidelines to minimize the passing options, while getting better position to guard the three-second area.

2. Defensive players should anticipate movements of the offensive players and move with cat-like quickness to guard them.

3. Force the ball to the side opposite your best rebounder.

4. Front a low-post player unless the player cannot shoot, then play baseline side or behind.

5. Play behind or ball side of a high-post player.

6. A player driving to the basket against the man-for-man defense should be stopped first, then the passing path must be cut off.

7. Players should be able to sag into the low-post area on a sideline perimeter pass within one second.

8. Take advantage of a baseline-sideline corner. Use it as another defensive player to trap the offensive man.

9. Discourage passes to a post-man by utilizing sagging-from-the-top tactics, then move out to guard the perimeter player receiving the next pass.

TIP 3

Quick Ball Possession With Full-Court Man-to-Man Pressure Stunts

OVERVIEW

The full-court man-for-man press can be an excellent primary defense. It is utilized in different ways depending upon the personnel available, the ability of the opposing players, the time period of the game, and the score. Generally a one-on-one press with limited innovations is advisable when a team is ahead. More emphasis is put on pressuring the opponent bringing the ball up-court than on trying to gain possession of the ball. Ball possessions usually come from violations by the ball handler rather than from interceptions, steals, or recoveries. This conservative employment of the press contains the opponent while still creating some advantages in using pressure.

However, there are times (for example, when the opponent is leading in the latter stages of the game) a team should use a more aggressive type press to get the ball. Another pressing situation is found where it is necessary to change the slow tempo of a game. Still another time is when the situation may call for trying to gain ball possession in a hurry on a temporary basis. There are aggressive tactics I call **stunts** that can help accomplish the quick-ball-possession goal. Stunts like individual defensive moves, trapping, and single jumps can tantalize the opponent into various turnovers. The success of the stunts depends to some degree on the teamwork by the players.

15

EXECUTION

There are four phases necessary to move the ball up-court when an offensive team is pressured full-court. The first one is to inbound the ball, the second is to move the ball into the offensive front court, the third is to look for a direct move to the basket for a shot, and the fourth is to set up an alignment in preparation to starting a patterned offense. The third step is often eliminated. However, this gives the defense an advantage to gamble more for the ball. The stunts that follow are geared for the defensive team to take the ball away before steps three or four.

    The first stunt, the Rover, is depicted in Diagram 3-1. The defense sets up in a full-court press with players X4 and X3 fronting their men. X2 does not guard O1 attempting to inbound the ball. Instead X2 drops back toward the top of the circle between the other players in the offensive backcourt and assumes the **Rover** position with the freedom to prevent or intercept a pass to either O3 or O2. In this case, the rover intercepts a pass intended for O2. Should O2 catch the ball, then X2 must guard O2 while X3 would

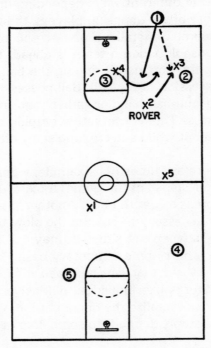

Diagram 3-1

help set a trap, making it necessary for X4 to guard O1. The alternative would be for X3 to pick up O1 and X4 to stay with O3. Meanwhile X5 would guard O4 and X1 would guard O5 with the Ball-You-Man rule discussed in Tip 2.

The second stunt is the Corner-trap-play (Diagram 3-2). The object is to play regular man-to-man prior to the inbound pass attempt, then trap in the corner when the ball is passed there. Player X2 takes a stance slightly to offensive player O1's right shoulder, forcing the pass to O2 in the corner. Players X2 and X3 trap O2 in the corner. An individual stunt can be made by X2 by taking four steps towards O2, then quickly moving backward to pick off a return pass attempt to O1 from O2. In the diagram, X4 moves in position ready to intercept a pass attempt to O1. Should the ball be passed successfully to O1 or O3, the defensive players should move quickly to pick up and guard the nearest player, one-on-one. Players X1 and X5's assignments are the same as on the previous play.

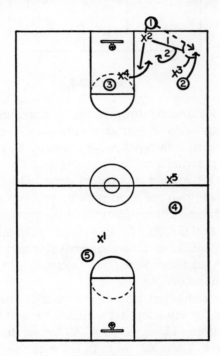

Diagram 3-2

The third stunt is the Run-and-jump (Diagram 3-3). This stunt can take place either in sequence with the first two or individually.

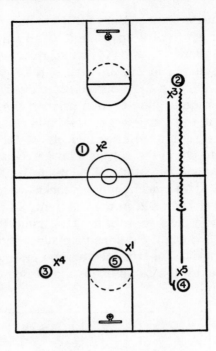

Diagram 3-3

In this case, the Run-and-jump stunt is depicted as follows: X3 permits O2 to dribble along the sidelines. As O2 enters the frontcourt moving at a fast pace, X5 leaves O4 and races to guard dribbler O2 (jump-switch), trying to force a ball handling mistake by O2. Meanwhile, X3 moves quickly to guard O4. If O2 stops dribbling, the defensive players then play a very competitive Ball-You-Man defense with intentions of intercepting a pass or forcing a jump ball between X5 and O2. The jump-switch could take place between players X2 and X3 if O2 dribbles towards the middle of the court. A jump-switch or a fake jump-switch can create problems for a weak or careless ball handler.

The Midcourt-sideline trap is the fourth stunt. This run and trap stunt is ideal for intercepting a lateral pass at midcourt, as well as forcing a violation. In Diagram 3-4, X3 forces dribbler O2 to move along the sidelines. Then X3 steps in front of the dribbler O2, forcing O2 to either cut back towards the middle or stop dribbling. Player X2 moves quickly over to set the midcourt-sideline trap with X3. Player X4 positions himself for a possible interception should O2 decide to pass to O1. (Although O3 is left unguarded, it is diffi-

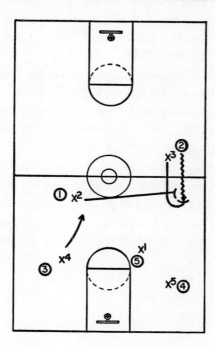

Diagram 3-4

cult for O2 to make an easy pass from the trap. X4 should stay in position to encourage a pass to O1.) If no interception is available, then X4 guards O1. Meanwhile, X1 must remain in the Ball-You-Man rule while guarding O5. A second choice is for X5 to trap O2 with X3's help, leaving X2 to guard O4. A third possibility would be for X5 to cross over to guard X2's man when X2 helps set a trap on O2, X4 would then guard O4. These stunting rotations are confusing to the opponent. Each forces the offense to make quick adjustments in a short time period, thereby increasing the chance for error.

COACHING POINTS

1. Try stunting periodically throughout the game to keep added pressure on the opponent.
2. Permit players to gamble in the defensive frontcourt, and to play more conservative in the backcourt when close to the basket.

3. Players should mix fakes in with the jumps or traps to keep the opponent off balance, and thereby give more opportunity to intercept passes.

4. Players should observe careless ball handling and seek ways to take advantage of the mistakes.

5. Force the ball away from the best ball handler, then make it difficult for this player to receive a return pass.

6. Use the midcourt lines, sidelines, or the corners in assisting the players to be more effective when jumping or trapping.

7. Pressure the ball handler into moving fast, then make a Run-and-jump forcing a quick change of direction or stop.

8. Develop a set of verbal as well as automatic signals for communication to insert the various stunts.

TIP 4

Simplifying Zone Pressure Trapping with the Three Trap Principles

OVERVIEW

In the past, the complexity of the zone presses made them very difficult to attack successfully. These defenses presented many obstacles to be overcome in order for a team to win consistently. But in recent times, offensive-minded coaches have been creative enough to develop press breakers that can overwhelm and defeat zone pressure defenses. Players' individual offensive abilities have improved immensely, making it easier to utilize the modern press-breaking offenses.

The zone presses may still have an impact on basketball. Most teams include at least one zone press in their defensive system. The strength of the press depends to some degree on how often efficient trapping takes place. Traps may be set anywhere on the court. It would be difficult to plan player movements to set each trap. You may think that there are many rules necessary for trapping. This is not true. Trapping is relatively simple, as we discovered after several seasons of zone pressing. It can be made simple with the use of three trap principles.

There are only three possible player alignments when trapping takes place, **no matter what zone press is utilized.** These three principles make it possible to successfully use the zone presses.

EXECUTION

The greatest value of the three trap principles is the opportunity to analyze immediately whether the alignments are set up with proper player positioning. A quick glance by each player is all it takes to verify correct positioning, and to locate and move to proper position when necessary. The basis for the three principles is the location of the ball in relation to the center court area, the sidelines, the corners, and the offensive basket.

Trap Principle 1: Two-on-the-Ball, Two-Floating-and-One-Back

Any trap that takes place in the center-court area and away from either sideline, has a 2-2-1 player alignment. Diagram 4-1 is an example of Principle 1, the center-court area trap. The player with the ball, O1, is being trapped away from the sidelines by X2 and X3. There are two floaters, X4 and X5, and X1 is the player in the back position.

The roles of each position are as follows: The trappers try to harass the trapped player into making a mistake. Should the player escape the trap, either trapper could guide the new ball handler into another trap, or look for a new position to fill in another trap situation.

The floater(s) look to intercept a pass, set up a trap, or take an unoccupied defensive position in another trap situation. The back player serves as a safety-man protecting the basket area.

Trap Principle 2: Two-on-the-Ball-One-Floating, One-in-Lane-and-One-Back

Whenever the ball is moved into a trap along either sideline away from the defensive back-court corner, the second trapping principle should be used. This is the Two-on-the-ball-one-floater-one-in-lane-and-one-back principle, as shown in Diagram 4-2. The player O1, with the ball, is trapped along the sideline immediately over midcourt by X2 and X3. Player X4 is the floater, X1 is the player in the lane (with floater responsibilities), and X5 serves as the safety-man.

Trap Principle 3: Two-on-the-Ball-One-Floater-Two-Side-by-Side

This third principle is in effect when the player with the ball is trapped in the offensive front court, in the sideline-baseline area. The following coverage takes place (Diagram 4-3). Players X2 and

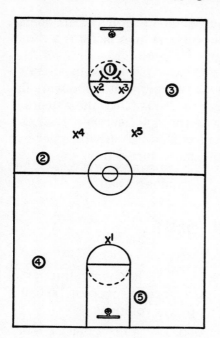

Diagram 4-1

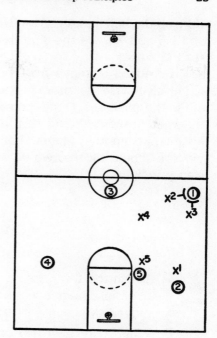

Diagram 4-2

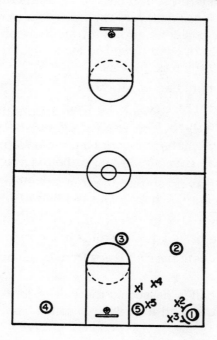

Diagram 4-3

X3 trap the ball handler O1 in the corner as X4 serves as the floater, and X5 and X1 are the side-by-side (safety) men along the three-second lane.

Rotations to move from one trap principle to another can be either clockwise, counter clockwise, or independent maneuvers filling in the positions. Once the safety position is filled, the players in the best position should stop or slow the ball handler's progress. Meanwhile, another player should help set a trap, and the other two players should fill the two vacant positions dictated by the proper trap principle.

COACHING POINTS

1. Teach the three trap principles and alignments, then practice these maneuvers by walking through each as the ball is moved up-court. Try various player rotations.

2. When playing a floater position, look to the Ball-You-Man rule (Tip 2) on a player in the area.

3. It is considered sound basketball to assign the safety position to a specific player. The other four players should fill in the other positions during a trap situation. The exact position would depend upon the location of the players on the court and their skill levels.

4. Players should anticipate trap situations and react quickly.

5. When a dribbler escapes a trap, any available player may guard and guide that player to another trap.

6. A coach might have players alternate trapping by first trapping in the baseline area and then in the sideline area.

7. The two players setting the trap should apply pressure, but take precautions not to foul the ball handler.

8. All players should be situated between the ball and the defensive basket as the ball is being maneuvered up-court.

9. Try to prevent passing lanes from being open to the trapped player.

10. When a ball is passed to the weakside, try to force both a sideline trap and a sideline-baseline trap.

TIP 5

Defensing the Internal Area

OVERVIEW

The strength of any defense evolves around stopping the opposition from taking shots near the basket, inasmuch as the prime offensive objective is to attempt high percentage shots. There are two ways to move closer to the basket for a shot attempt. First, there is the transition game—fast-breaking after a rebound, after a basket, after steals, after interceptions, or after recoveries. These should take place prior to a set defense. The second method is for the team with the ball to set up a pattern which will permit the offense to move closer to the basket. Patterns are built on the theory of "inside-out scoring." Both methods are equally important, although significantly more time is spent in developing various patterns to counter a variety of defenses.

This tip deals with defensing the internal (inside) area when the offense is playing pattern basketball. The Internal Area referred to here is inside the three-second lane, the high-post, the side-post, and the low-post positions, just outside the lane.

In order to defend this area properly with a man-to-man defense, each player must be able to guard an opposing player 1-on-1, and then must receive help from other player(s) when needed. In other words, it is necessary to use not only the individual but also the team concepts of defense. Pressure by a defensive man on the ball handler is a most important factor, since this makes it difficult for the ball handler to execute drives, or might cause errant passes by the offense. Pressure will also thwart the efforts to initiate the patterns correctly. It might also affect the timing as the offensive pattern is being executed.

The zone defenses also use the individual coverage principles to some degree, as well as the team-type defenses. These principles are in effect when the ball enters into an individual player's zone.

EXECUTION

In order to defend the internal area successfully, it is mandatory to defense the following offensive plays:

1. A player executing a quick move and shot near the basket
2. A player driving toward the basket
3. A player cutting to the basket to receive a pass in the internal zone
4. A player receiving a pass in the internal zone.

Man-to-Man Defense
in the Internal Area

Defensing cutters with man-to-man coverage is accomplished by the Ball-You-Man rule discussed in Tip 2. It is used by players guarding opponents away from the ball. The Ball-You-Basket rule (Tip 2) is used by the man guarding the ball handler. Diagram 5-1 illustrates three keys to guarding the internal area. First is the team alignment with extra pressure on the player with the ball and the other four players in or near the internal area. Second, the players on defense should stay in line with the ball. The further the offensive man is from the ball, the more distance the defensive player

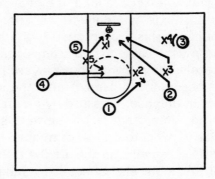

Diagram 5-1

may drop off his opponent. Third, the Ball-You-Man rule must be used to defense all cutters (defensive player may face the cutters or the ball). This defensive tactic takes place against any alignment with the ball on the side of the court.

The proper defensive alignment and defensing of cutters is depicted in the diagram, with X4 putting pressure on ball handler O3, while X3 guards O2. Player X1 guards O5 from inside the lane, as does X5 guarding O4, while X2 guards O1. From this internal area protective alignment, each defensive player guards his opponent against a cut by staying between the ball and the offensive player.

The Ball-You-Man rule is applicable when defending against a post-player by preventing him from receiving a pass. The only difference is the position of the defender in relation to the location of the ball. Diagram 5-2 shows how the post coverage would take place with the ball in three different locations. With the ball at the top of the circle, player X1 is at the side of O5. Player X1 should keep his left arm in between the ball and his opponent.

On the right and left side posts, X1 is playing on the baseline side of O5. With O5 at the right and left low-post positions, X1 fronts O5 unless O5 is a poor offensive player; in that case X1 plays behind O5.

Diagram 5-3 shows the defense stopping the low-post man's attempt to drive to the basket. If O5 receives a pass in the low-post position and makes a move to the middle of the lane, the remaining defensive players collapse toward the basket to prevent the progress or the shot. Player O5 is in the heart of the defense and will suffer the consequence of playing against two or more opponents.

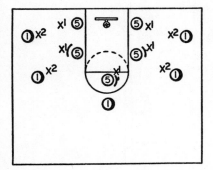

Diagram 5-2

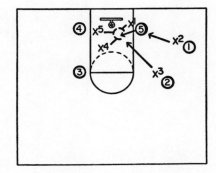

Diagram 5-3

Diagram 5-3 displays the action employed. Low post-man O5 with the ball drives toward the basket guarded by X1. X5 in the meantime moves in first to block O5's move, while X2, X3, and X4 move into position to stop further penetration or a pass out to a teammate. The rule to protect is to first "stop the shot, then cover the passing lanes." This forces the three-second violation by O5, and prevents a pass to a teammate for an easy shooting attempt.

The Spider Trap

This trap is set where the three-second lane and the baseline meet on either side of the court. It can lead to a turnover with alert defensive team play. Diagram 5-4 shows how to defense the 1-on-1 drive by forcing the ball handler into a Spider trap. With the right side of the court cleared, driver O1 makes a 1-on-1 move to the basket. The defensive man, X2, forces O1 away from the basket to the three-second line-baseline area on the right side. Meanwhile, X3 follows O1 from behind. When X2 stops O1's drive, X3 assists X2 in setting a trap on O1. The remainder of the defensive players should move toward the ball into the three-second area. Player X4 should be alert to intercept the ball, should O1 attempt to pass back to O2.

This Spider trap may be initiated any time a player dribbles into that area. The important points are to set the trap, to prevent a pass to the three-second lane, then to attempt to pick off the pass made out of the trap area.

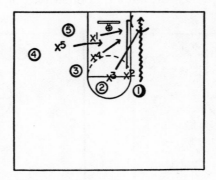

Diagram 5-4

Zones Against Internal Scoring

Protecting the internal area by switching to a zone is a good tactic to use to offset the opposition's size advantage, style of play, or the ability to play well inside by individual players. Zones are geared to discourage inside play-action and force a team to shoot from the outside. A well-coached offensive team should combine good out-side shooting with inside movement and good passing to get within the defensive area.

To have an effective zone defense, the ball should generally be forced to either side of the key. Each type of zone is in a similar alignment in attempting to prevent the ball from being moved to the top of the free throw circle. The coverage is to prevent a pass to the inside or to prevent the ball on the inside from coming to the out-side. This is the same as in 1-3-1 alignment (Tip 2). With all players collapsing into the lane and using the Ball-You-Man rule, the Ball-You-Basket rule is used to put pressure on the ball handler with one defensive player, while the other four guard the lane area. With proper sagging and individual man responsibility, the zone, with combination man and zone maneuvers, can be a very effective de-fense for protecting the internal area.

COACHING POINTS

1. Players should always be conscious of the internal zone coverage.

2. **Stop the drive, and attempt to intercept passes in the passing lane** is a vital two-step sequence.

3. A defense should generally "flatten out" when the player with the ball moves towards the baseline.

4. Each player should be guarding his opponent in addition to being ready to move into the internal area to guard or help guard another player.

5. All players should be taught how to defense a player in the three post positions.

6. Try to secure an advantageous rebounding position in order to limit opponents to a single shot.

7. When a team is shooting well from the outside court, try harder to obtain more interceptions and rebounds. Don't give opponents any easy baskets.

8. Use the Spider trap often, especially when using the zone defenses.

TIP 6

Combating Internal Area Screens

OVERVIEW

The improvement in player offensive fundamentals makes it more difficult to play man-to-man defense. The Passing game and the One-four stack can put an extra-heavy burden on a defense. Both types of offenses feature considerable screening to free a player to use his offensive skill in high percentage shooting areas. The screening is done simultaneously and/or consecutively by three or four players in different locations. Multiple screening usually takes place in the heart of the defense or the internal area defined in Tip 5.

In order for a team to use a man-to-man defense effectively, it is a top priority for players to be well-schooled in how to combat offensive screens, particularly in the internal area. Guarding the ball handler closely and forcing him away from the screening action is also extremely important.

The defensive team should be able to combat on-the-ball screens (screen-and-roll plays) as well as off-the-ball screens. A variety of individual defensive plays along with help by teammates not being screened are the two essentials for protecting against screens in both the perimeter and internal areas. Switching to a zone defense may be the best way to combat multiple screens, but even a zone defense is vulnerable to some screening plays.

EXECUTION

The underlying cardinal rule to playing any defense successfully is that each player **must be schooled** in man-to-man principles. It is an easy task to apply these principles to a zone defense.

31

Defensive Man-to-Man Screening

An individual's responsibility in combating a screen includes mastering the following three maneuvers:

1. The over-the-top, or staying close to an opponent while fighting off screening attempts by any player.
2. Switching of defensive assignments with a teammate after being screened.
3. The slide-through, or staying with an opponent by moving through an area made available by a teammate when a screen is attempted.

If players are skilled in the three maneuvers it is possible to guard opponents regardless of the offensive formation or pattern movements. Anticipation, alertness and teamwork are the important ingredients.

There are four types of screens which may be used. They are the following:

1. The **down-screen,** where the screener faces the baseline area.
2. The **up-screen,** where the screener faces midcourt.
3. The **inside-lateral screen,** where the screener faces the sideline on his half of the court.
4. The **outside-lateral screen,** where the screener faces the three-second lane.

Examples of the three maneuvers and the four screens are shown in Diagrams 6-1, 6-2, 6-3, and 6-4. All defensive assignments are made with the Ball-You-Basket rule when guarding a ballhandler, and Ball-You-Man rule when guarding a man off the ball as discussed in Tip 2.

In Diagram 6-1, O1 has the ball at the top and on the right side of the internal area. Player O3 sets an up-screen for O2, who takes a jab step left, then cuts toward the basket on the right side. (A jab step helps an offensive player run a defensive opponent into the screen.) Meanwhile, X4 handling O3 switches to cover O2. Player X3 switches to guard O3 after being screened by O3.

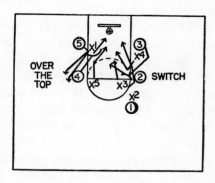

Diagram 6-1

Looking at the left side of the diagram, O4 sets a down-screen on X1 permitting O5 to take a jab step left then moving right up the side of the lane. Player O4 moves to the basket after setting the screen, and is being guarded by X5. Player X1 then fights his way over the top of the screen to stay with O5.

In Diagram 6-2, with O1 possessing the ball at the top of the free throw circle, O3 sets an inside-lateral screen on X3, giving O2 an opportunity to jab-step left, then move right towards the basket. Player X4 makes a switch to guard O2's cut, while X3 switches to guard O3 (right side court action).

On the left side, O4 sets an outside-screen on X1 permitting O5 to jab-step left, then move towards the left sideline. Player O4 moves toward the basket guarded by X1, after a defensive switch with X5, who now guards O5.

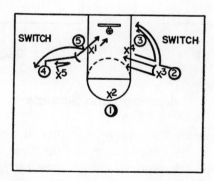

Diagram 6-2

The technique of breaking up the shuffle-cut rub-off screens is depicted in Diagram 6-3. Player O1 passes to O2, who in turn relays it to O3. Player O1 jab-steps left, then makes a cut to the right attempting to run X2 into screener O5. Player X2 slides through the area between O5 and X1 to stay with O1, who cuts on the other side of O5. The second cutter, O2, jab-steps right, then cuts left of O5 while his guard X3 also attempts to slide through between O5 and X1.

A clear-out, screen-and-roll situation is outlined in Diagram 6-4. Players O3, O5, and O4 move to the left side, permitting O2 to set up an inside-lateral screen on X2 for O1, who has the ball. O1 dribbles off screener O2, who then rolls toward the basket. Player X3 switches to stop dribbler O1, and X2 switches to guard O2.

Meanwhile, on the left side, O5, from a wing position, sets an outside-lateral screen on X4, guarding low post-man O3, freeing O3 to move to a wing position. Player X4 switches to guard O5, trying to roll to the basket and X1 switches to pick up O3. Player X5 drops back to help out in the internal area.

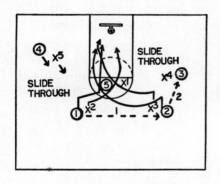

Diagram 6-3

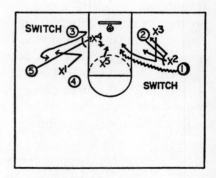

Diagram 6-4

Defensing Zone Screens

There is usually limited screening attempted against a zone defense. Most screens are geared to trap a baseline defensive player. The baseline screen takes place when the ball is on either sideline, forcing the zone into a 1-3-1 defensive alignment (Tip 2).

Diagram 6-5 shows how to stop the weakside-baseline screen play. With O1 possessing the ball, O4 sets a screen on X5, the weakside baseline defensive man. Player O1 passes to O5, who then

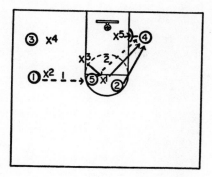

Diagram 6-5

passes to O2, standing behind screener O4. Meanwhile, X1 sees the play and moves quickly to cover O2. Player X3 can replace X1 to protect the vacated zone, while X1 should remain in that zone. Player X5 assumes the middle position between the ball and the basket.

COACHING POINTS

1. Players should anticipate multi-screens and avoid them by moving away from the screener's intended path.
2. If a player is not being screened, he should move to a position in line with the ball to help defend that area.
3. Use hedging (slowing down a teammate's opponent dribbling the ball, which permits the defensive man to re-establish a defensive position). This tactic minimizes switching on defense.
4. Use over-the-top guarding as a primary choice whenever possible.
5. Verbal help by a teammate is vital to avoid screens.
6. Be aware of ball location when fighting off screens on the weak side.
7. Be especially aware of switches made in the immediate area of the basket in order to prevent the opponents from scoring easy baskets.
8. **Keep pressure on the ball handler at all times** when defensing multiple screens.

TIP 7

Defensing the Weakside Plays

OVERVIEW

For scoring power, a team must utilize an offense that opens up avenues of scoring from the top of the free throw circle area, from the strong side (side of the ball), and from the weak side. Scoring attempts from the top and strong side are common for most teams, while weakside attempts are minimal. However, there is a growing trend to improve weakside offensive play. There should be a balance of scoring opportunities from each location because the threat of a strong weakside attack strengthens the offense immeasurably by forcing the defense to make adjustments which can make it more vulnerable. Weakside play minimizes the defensive overplay on the strong side and makes opportunities available for a quick pass inside for a lay-up, or for an open weakside attempt at the basket. Since the weakside play is a major part of any offense, weakside defensing also becomes extremely important.

EXECUTION

Sound weakside defensive coverage has four rules. These rules are practical for both man-to-man and the zone defenses: (1) There must be pressure on the player with the ball; (2) Try to prevent the ball from being passed to an offensive player coming into the three-second area, thereby forcing the ball around the perimeter; (3) Block the passing lanes to limit perimeter passing; and (4) Rush out to challenge the weakside opponent receiving a pass. Attempt to protect the internal area while the whole defensing process is taking place.

There is a difference in types of offense opportunities when a defensive team plays man-to-man or zone. In man-to-man, there may be more room to move because the offense may be clearing an area by multiple screening, by moving players away from the basket for a 1-on-1 drive, or by spreading for the purpose of using a specific offense. There may not be any weakside help. However, in a zone defense there should be a player in position to attack the weakside offensive opponent(s) with teammate help available in the internal zone.

Man-to-Man Weakside Coverage

The Weakside crash (back-door) used by most teams should be planned for defensively as standard procedure. Diagram 7-1 depicts the defensing action against this maneuver. Player O2 has the ball near the top of the free throw circle on the right side of the court; he passes to O3, who quickly moves into the high-post position after post-man O5 moves to the right side near the baseline. Meanwhile, O1 starts moving right, then cuts toward the basket on the weakside. Defensing this play involves stopping O3 from receiving the pass at the post, or preventing O1 from receiving a pass from O3. If O3 receives the pass successfully, then X4 should guard on O3's left to prevent the pass to O1. If O1 receives a pass, then X2 should cut off any attempt for O1 to move to the basket. Players X1 and X5 should sag to help out in case X2 is out of position to stop O1.

A second play against a weakside play takes place with the post-man receiving a quick pass (as shown in Diagram 7-2). It is less difficult to pass the ball to a weakside player once the post-man receives the ball. Player O1 passes to post-man O5, who then relays to O3. Player O3 can pass to O4, drive to the basket, or shoot. Defensing this play entails stopping the pass to O3, or for X4 to guard O3 immediately after he receives the pass. While X5 moves to front the low post-man O4, a quick sagging movement by X3, X1, and X2 discourages any inside offensive play.

The third play focuses on defensing weakside screening, as shown in Diagram 7-3. Player O5 receives a pass and is defensed by his opponent X1, who moves to the O5's right to contest a weakside pass; meanwhile, O3 sets up an outside-lateral screen on X3 to permit O2 to move outside for a short jump shot. Player X3 should make a switch to guard O3 while X4 switches to guard O2. Player X5 should drop back into the middle to help if needed. If O2 sets an

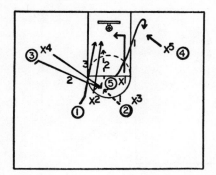

Diagram 7-1

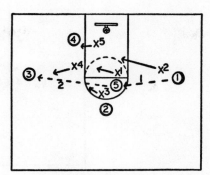

Diagram 7-2

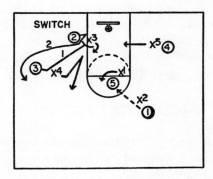

Diagram 7-3

inside screen (see Tip 6), then X4 should fight over the top of the screen or switch with X3. Meanwhile, X1 and X5 should sag to cover the inside.

Zone Defense Weakside Coverage

Zone weakside coverage also evolves around the four weakside defensing rules. The most difficult task is to stop a quick shot from the wing or side position on the court. With the ball on one side of the court, the zones should be in a 1-3-1 alignment (Tip 2). The weakside wing-man pass is usually possible by a direct pass from the strongside wing player (O2) to the player in the weakside wing area (O3). Diagram 7-4 shows how to defense this play. Player O2 has the ball on the wing forcing the 1-3-1 zone alignment. Player X2 rushes to defense O3 as the rest of the players set up a 1-3-1

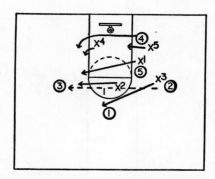

Diagram 7-4

alignment on the opposite side of the court. Player X1 is in the middle of the court, X4 on the left wing, X3 is on the right wing, and X5 is in the swing position near the basket. Should X4 gamble for an interception, X1 would move down to cover the vacated zone, X2 would take X1's zone, and X3 would replace X2.

COACHING POINTS

1. Force poor passes by situating players in or near passing lanes to slow down ball movement to the weakside, thereby permitting time for defensive re-alignment.

2. Any player defending an opponent on an inside zone pass must be aware of weakside offensive player movements.

3. Attempt to discourage a pass or drive by the opponents; also try to stop a shot attempt when rushing to defend against a weakside player.

4. When a low-post player receives a pass, be aware of how to prevent a weakside pass attempt.

5. The "Ball-You-Man" and "Ball-You-Basket" rules (Tip 2) must be used in any defense to stop weakside plays.

6. Try to force a weakside player out of his shooting area by anticipating a pass and covering him quickly.

7. Drill the team often on stopping weakside action by having the defensive players play with their arms behind their backs, which forces good foot work, positioning, and anticipation.

8. Players should move on every pass for better positioning.

TIP 8

Recognizing the Proper Situations To Take the Offensive Charge

OVERVIEW

The offensive charge is advantageous to the defensive team because it is a personal foul on the charging player, who also is penalized by loss of ball possession or the one-and-one free throw by the player fouled. It is discouraging to suffer an offensive turnover when it occurs during an offensive thrust to the basket. A charging foul occurs when the defensive man establishes a floor position and is pushed or charged by an offensive player. An offensive charge can be made by a player with or without the ball who cannot stop in time to avoid contact. The basis for this is contact caused by excessive speed, carelessness, or bad footwork.

A charging foul can occur anywhere on the court but usually takes place in the offensive team's front court, within twenty-five feet of the basket. The more defensive players clustered together, the better opportunity for a charging foul. Situations are more often present during the transition game, the offensive pattern movements (such as after a player passes the ball), after a shot, or when rebounding. Most offensive fouls are set up by a "switch" in defensive coverage by two players, while others might result from individual 1-on-1 coverage. Also, defensive charging fouls are more common when a team plays man-to-man defense than when playing a zone type defense.

EXECUTION

Diagrams 8-1 through 8-6 depict the various on and off the ball, individual and switching, which cause the offensive charging situation.

41

Diagram 8-1 shows X2 guiding O1, who is dribbling along the left sideline towards X3. X3 steps to his left, establishes defensive position, and is charged by the dribbler. X2 switches to guard O2. (A speeding dribbler trying to get past his man enroute to the basket is the ideal player to set up for a charging foul.)

In Diagram 8-2, dribbler O1 tries to drive the three-second lane. Player O1 appears to be beating defensive player X2 when X1, guarding low-post player O5, establishes a defensive position in O1's path and is thereby charged by O1. In the meantime, X2 should switch to guard O5.

Diagram 8-3 shows another switch-charge situation. This time the charge is made at the top of the free throw circle. O1 dribbles to his right, then passes to O2 moving behind O1. Immediately after the pass, O2 collides with X2, who switches to establish a defensive position on new dribbler O2. Meanwhile, X3 establishes a defensive position on O1 and is ready to take an off-the-ball offensive charge should O1 get careless in his movements.

The changing of direction with a spin dribble is the situation displayed in Diagram 8-4. Player O1 dribbles right, executes a spin dribble to the left, while X2 establishes a defensive position to set up the offensive charging situation. Another ball-handling charge situation is shown on the same diagram on the right side of the court. An explanation will follow later.

In Diagram 8-5, low post-man O5 makes a driving move toward the basket, takes a shot, then makes contact with X1; therefore, X1 had beaten O5 to a position near the basket and had established a proper defensive position.

An offensive charge after a pass from a fast break with a 3-2 triangle situation is shown in Diagram 8-6. When X2 establishes a defensive position in O1's path, O1 passes the ball and charges into X2 and commits an offensive foul.

The off-the-ball charge situations are drawn out in Diagrams 8-4, 8-5 and 8-7. Even a weakside exchange can cause an offensive charge situation. This is displayed on the right side of the court in Diagram 8-4, where O3 weakside exchanges with O4. Player X5 establishes a defensive position in O3's path and draws the charging foul.

The charging foul by a player moving to the basket for a rebound is shown on the left side of Diagram 8-5. In the right side action, O5 is shown making a move in, then taking a shot. Player O2 on the left side attempts to make a quick move to establish a re-

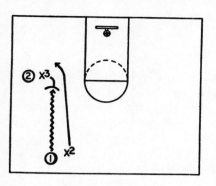

Diagram 8-1

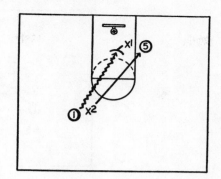

Diagram 8-2

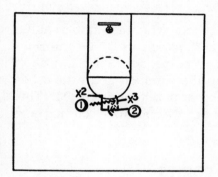

Diagram 8-3

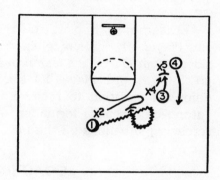

Diagram 8-4

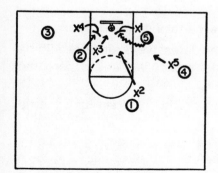

Diagram 8-5

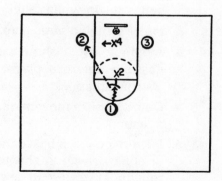

Diagram 8-6

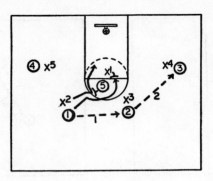

Diagram 8-7

bounding position. Player X4, who is guarding O3, sees the move and quickly establishes a defensive position on O2 and is charged by O2.

Diagram 8-7 depicts a charge situation which can stop a shuffle cut. Player O2, after receiving the ball, passes to O3 on the right side. Player O1 makes a shuffle cut off post-man O5, forcing X2 to go to O5's right. Player X1 sizes up the situation and establishes defensive position to receive the charging foul from O1. This cutting-type charge formation may be used in many cutting and screening situations off the ball.

COACHING POINTS

1. Charge techniques include protecting oneself with arms and hands to cushion body contact, falling backward immediately upon contact, and learning to cushion the fall with palms down when falling to the floor.

2. Players should anticipate charge-taking situations.

3. A definite establishment of the defensive position should be possible before a player attempts to assume a potential charge situation.

4. Quick, cat-like movements are necessary to set up a charge situation.

5. Players near the basket can draw many charging fouls on a dribbler driving, a shooter before and after shooting, or a rebounder trying to assume position or jumping into a player.

6. When a player receives an offensive charge, teammates should continue playing until the referee terminates play.

7. Avoid careless misuse of receiving the charge, as the contact might cause injury.

8. Offensive players who appear to be vulnerable to committing offensive fouls should be identified by both the coach and the players.

TIP 9

Improve Defensive Rebounding With Floor Spot Positions

OVERVIEW

Over 50 percent of the shots attempted in a basketball game are missed. Approximately 15 to 20 percent of the points scored by a team are made on second shot attempts. Therefore, the old cliche "eliminate second shots to win" is true. This is especially true since the average difference between winning and losing games is fewer than ten points.

Spot rebounding from both the man-to-man and zone defense is better than the conventional "block-out and go to the basket" technique. In spot rebounding, the defensive players should leave their opponent on any shot attempt and fill in rebound positions near the basket. Boxing out (or "blocking out") takes place within the spots to maintain positioning prior to jumping to retrieve a missed shot.

The elimination of blocking out prior to assuming spot positions allows for quicker movement to the basket to beat the opponent to the spot and to therefore have more time to prepare for the jump. More time is available to use crisscross tactics to gain inside rebounding position on offensive players. Blocking out players more than six feet from the basket is not considered a good policy, as it permits other opponents to secure better rebounding positions closer to the basket while the blocking-out process takes place. Movements such as pivots and spins to gain inside position in the designated spots are necessary within eight feet of the basket. Once in a proper position, blocking out or fighting for positioning is vital in helping to secure the rebound. Player height and jumping ability are important, but proper positioning is the key to outstanding rebounding.

47

EXECUTION

By doing a study on the direction missed shots bounced off the rim, our staff discovered that when a ball is shot from either baseline or corner, 60 percent of the shots bounced back towards the shooter, while 30 percent bounced to the opposite side of the court. Ten percent bounced to the middle when a shot was attempted from either side of the basket away from baseline, 50 percent of the misses bounced towards the shooter, 40 percent towards the opposite side away from the baseline, and 10 percent bounced towards either corner. When the ball was shot from the top of the free throw circle, 60 percent rebounded towards the shooter, 35 percent to either side away from the baseline, and 5 percent towards either corner. Although the study was limited, we did realize some interesting tendencies. It gave us some credence to continue using the spot position method of rebounding. We also had a better idea on which direction the ball was more likely to bounce. Another point should be taken into consideration. Seeing the ball in flight helps a player sense which way the ball will bounce off the rim. This enables him to move or jump at the angle in which he can retrieve more rebounds.

Diagram 9-1 depicts the four rebounding spots. Spot A is the middle area immediately in front of the basket area, spots B and C are areas on either side of the basket, and spot D is the area at the free throw line. Spot D should be filled by two players, while the other spots require only one.

The order of spots occupied by players depends on the location of the shot attempted. If the shot is taken from either baseline or corner areas, the spot opposite the shooting area should be filled first, then the middle spot, and then the spot on the same side, which is covered last, because 60 percent of the shots bounce **back** towards a baseline corner shooter. The player guarding him moves slowly towards the spot on his side of the basket to retrieve high rebounds. Players in the opposite and middle spots have a good chance to move or jump at the proper angle because they have a better view of the ball in flight. The D zone should be filled last.

If the ball is shot from the side away from the baseline, the middle spot should be filled first, followed by the side opposite the shot, and finally the side of the shot. The D spot again should be occupied last.

When the ball is shot from the top of the circle, the middle spot is filled first, followed by the sides to be determined by the angle of the shot, with the D position filled last.

Spot Rebounding from a Man-to-Man Defense

Diagram 9-2 shows players filling the rebound spots on a right side baseline shot. Player O3 attempts the shot from the right corner, and X1 goes to the basket side opposite the shot. Player X5 fills the middle position, X3 the spot on the shot attempt side, and X1 the free throw position. Meanwhile, X4 moves toward the basket watching for a high rebound.

Player O2 attempts the shot from the right side away from the baseline in Diagram 9-3. Player X1 takes the middle position, X4 the opposite side spot, X5 the same side spot, and X2 the free throw line spot. In the meantime, X3 moves toward the basket to the D spot to retrieve a possible high carom in that area.

Diagram 9-4 shows a crisscross move to give a defensive rebounder the inside position on an offensive rebounder already established in a side spot. The rest of the action depicts filling the

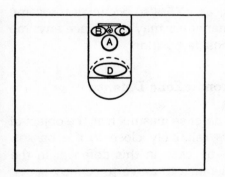

Diagram 9-1

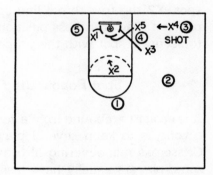

Diagram 9-2

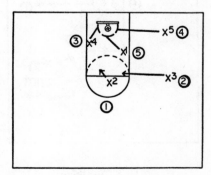

Diagram 9-3

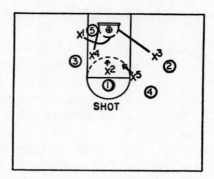

Diagram 9-4

other spots on a shot taken from the middle-court area. Player O1 shoots from the free throw line, as X4 takes a position in front of O5 (who has inside position on X1) on the left side spot. Player X1 crosses over to the middle spot, while X3 assumes the right side spot, X2 the free throw line spot, and X5 also occupies the same position. The crisscross position maneuver may take place anytime to secure a spot with the proper inside position.

Spot Rebounding From a Zone Defense

It is easier to rebound from a zone defense inasmuch as the object of a zone is to keep several players relatively close to the basket. Crisscross maneuvering also may be used in this defense. In the zone, players usually have less distance to move to occupy spots, giving them more time to use these types of tactics.

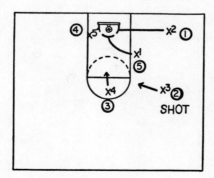

Diagram 9-5

Diagram 9-5 demonstrates how to fill in the positions when the ball is shot from a side position away from the baseline against a zone 1-3-1 defensive alignment (Tip 2). Player O2 takes the shot from the right side, so X5 fills the spot on the opposite side, X1 the center position, X2 the same side spot, and X4 the free throw line position. Player X3 follows the shot, then stays in the free throw line spot.

COACHING POINTS

1. To rebound a lay-up drive attempt, the nearest player should move to fill in the middle position.

2. All five players should drive hard for **every rebound.**

3. Use a forward or reverse pivot move to fight for inside position against an offensive player established in a spot when the crisscross is not possible.

4. If a defensive player cannot secure an inside position, then keep opponent busy trying to block out in order that he will not be in position to jump for the ball.

5. Use crisscross maneuvers often to attempt to secure an inside position.

6. The player(s) at the free throw spot should look for the high rebounds and the loose ball recoveries.

7. Rebounders close to the basket should be ready to recover deflected balls when rebounds bounce into another area.

8. Players off the ball should anticipate a shot and move to a spot the instant the ball leaves the shooter's hand in order to secure the rebound.

TIP 10

The Transition Game With The Two Fast-Break Phases

OVERVIEW

The transition game is the action that takes place between the time a defensive team gains possession of the ball until the formal offensive pattern begins. The transition break is the two-phase attack that takes place following ball possession, after made or missed field goals, and free throw attempts. It also occurs following a steal, a recovery, or an intercepted pass, and lasts until the formal offensive pattern begins to form.

There should be two distinct phases in the transition break, with the objective being to score as quickly as possible before the opponent can set up a defense. It can be accomplished with a systematic progression in two phases.

The first phase is the **fast break.** Move the ball up-court quickly by outnumbering the opponent with 1-on-0, 2-on-1, 3-on-2, or 4-on-3 patterns. Time is an important factor in this phase. The action from possession to the shot attempt is geared to take up to five seconds. A quick lightening-like thrust and shot at the basket is the goal. The delayed fast break is the second phase, which begins after the initial fast break ceases. It occurs at a time when the defensive players have apparently stopped the offensive thrust and are looking to set up a drop-back defense, while the offensive players move into positions ready to begin the formal offensive pattern. The offensive team should utilize this interim period to strike quickly in an attempt to score. There are up to five valuable seconds in this phase of the attack. Ideally, all players should be capable of scoring. If a shot is not available or taken, then the ball should be passed to the floor leader, who moves to the perimeter into a position ready to begin the formal team offensive pattern to combat the drop-back defense.

By using the two-phase transition break, a team develops a continuity attack that finds players positioned ready to shoot the close shots if available, and then from the perimeter area, if necessary. The organization of this attack also offers excellent offensive rebounding positioning because players are near the basket. There are also players in position to play defense in case the ball is lost to the opponent.

EXECUTION

The two-phase break is geared to create a shot within a ten-second period by taking advantage of a slow or careless defensive retreat by the opponent. Because of the brief time allotment, it is unimportant whether a defensive team uses a zone or a man-for-man retreat. The attack is designed to beat either defense before there is time to set up.

In the fast-break phase, the first thrust depends to some degree upon where the ball is secured. If it is recovered in the offensive backcourt, perhaps only one quick pass to a player near the basket is necessary for a dribble and a shot. A recovery or defensive rebound would necessitate a longer pass, more passes, or several maneuvers to bring the ball toward the offensive end of the court.

For consistency in explaining the attack, let's assume that the ball has been rebounded off the defensive board, then moved upcourt quickly to the top of the free throw circle near the offensive basket. The object at this point is to outnumber the opposition, such as with a 2-on-1 attack.

If this is not possible, it is standard procedure to dribble the ball to the middle of the court and to prepare a triangle for a 3-on-2 or a 4-on-3 attack. The ball handler is near the free throw line and the wing-men positions are on either side of the basket immediately outside of the three-second area. The important point is that scoring opportunities become available by players making movements when occupying the triangle positions at the termination of the fast break.

Diagrams 10-1 and 10-2 depict the two different triangle alignments. They also indicate trailer movements which lead to a trailer shooting as well as creating shots for the other players.

Diagram 10-1 shows the Closed-triangle alignment. Along with O1 handling the ball at the free throw area, players O2 on the left wing and O3 on the right wing form the triangle. The Closed-triangle name was adopted for the reason that the wing men are immediately outside of the three second lane. In the Closed-triangle, when trailer O4 reaches the top of the circle, he shouts "trailer," then fakes a cut toward the basket, then moves behind O3 on the right side of the court. (The same maneuver could take place to the left.) There are now three players along the baseline within ten feet of the basket. This is called a Triangle-and-one. Meanwhile, player O5 remains in the safety position beyond the top of the circle near the offensive end.

The Open-triangle is shown in Diagram 10-2. This triangle is spread out with the purpose of giving more room under the basket for a scoring thrust. The wing men O2 and O3 are approximately eighteen feet from the basket. The following action takes place when O1 has the ball in the free throw line area. Trailer O4 then shouts "trailer" as he slows down near the top of the free throw circle area, then proceeds to blast up the middle of the lane for a pass from O1. If none is available, O4 assumes the right side low-post position, since he has cut to the basket on the right of O1 to form the Triangle-and-one, with O5 as the safety-man. (This play could also be run to the left.)

Some of the scoring opportunities with the wide triangle are as follows. Player O1 could drive the middle, with trailer O4 receiving a direct pass from O1. Either O2 or O3 could shoot a jump shot. Players O2 or O3 could pass into a post position to O4, who in turn

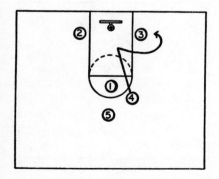

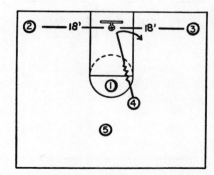

Diagram 10-1   **Diagram 10-2**

can occupy the low-post if the ball is moved from one side to the other. Player O4 should follow the ball if he does not receive a pass from O1.

If the shot is not taken, then the Phase two delay fast break begins. The delayed break can take place from either of the triangle alignments. The basic play in the delay break is shown in Diagram 10-3. (In this case, the Closed triangle is shown.) O1 has the ball near the free throw line area. Players O3 and O4 move up towards the free throw line. Meanwhile, O2 begins to move up, and sets an up-screen at the free throw line on the left side for O5 to cut. O1 passes to O4, who turns to face the basket for a possible shot. (Player O1 could have passed to O3 also.) Just as O4 receives the ball, safety-man O5 cuts to the basket off the up-screen set by player O2. Player O2 then moves into the free throw lane for a possible pass. In this diagram, O4 passes to O5 in front of the basket.

A variation of this manuever would be to have O5 set a down-screen for O2 at the block. Player O2 would move up the lane for a pass and O5 could roll to the basket. Player O5 could also set a down-screen for O3 on the right side with the same action taking place.

The delayed fast break off a Wide-triangle is shown in Diagram 10-4. Ball handler O1 is near the free throw line as O5 cuts towards the free throw lane, then sets a down screen to free O4, who moves into the middle for a pass. If O4 is not clear, then O4 continues to the left side low-post position. Player O1 passes to O3 in the right corner, who in turn passes to the low-post player O5. It is possible for O1 to pass to O2, who could pass to O4 in the left low-post. If

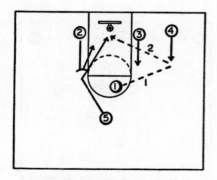

Diagram 10-3

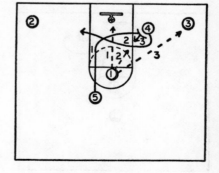

Diagram 10-4

neither O5 or O4 are open, with O3 handling the ball a pass back to O1, who in turn can pass to O2 on the left side for the jump shot, or a pass to O4 at the low-post.

If no shot is taken after five seconds, then the player with the ball should pass it to O1 for a move out to the top of the circle ready to begin the formal pattern. This would then terminate the transition break.

COACHING POINTS

1. Move fast but under control when attempting to execute the transition break. Be patient and execute the proper movements for both phases, looking for an inside shot or a jumper with players in good rebounding positions.

2. There are several shot opportunities on each basic maneuver. A player should be ready to receive a pass, then drive to the basket, or shoot a baby (short) jump shot.

3. Wing men should stay out of the three-second lane when setting up the Closed-triangle.

4. A trailer moving in to shoot on the Wide-triangle should maintain body balance in order to stop or change direction without charging into a defensive man.

5. A ball handler at the free throw line area should attempt to keep dribbling the ball until ready to pass, shoot, or move out to start the pattern offense.

6. Any player near the basket should be ready to shoot immediately after receiving the ball. Occasionally a fake shot followed by some type of regular shot is in order.

7. Many baskets off the fast break are scored by a player rebounding a missed shot.

8. During the delayed fast break, look for inside passes if a defensive player carelessly shifts to a different opponent or to a different area of a zone defense.

Variations of the Phase One Triangle And Player Maneuvers

OVERVIEW

Vary the Phase one conventional fast break triangle and the Triangle-and-one for better shot opportunities. Using the closed and open triangle also changes the size of the offensive structure, thereby creating defensive problems. The asymmetrical triangle is a triangle that inclines toward one side or the other and offers a new variation as well as new problems for the defense.

There are also various player maneuvers to help form the triangles. These maneuvers serve to clear a wing area, to clear the area in front of the basket, or to clear the free throw line area, besides clearing areas for a player to fill for a quick shot as screening plays are being executed.

EXECUTION

There are two maneuvers that should be used from the conventional Closed triangle. The first is the Single-cross (Diagram 11-1). Player O1 has the ball in the free throw circle area. The triangle is set up with O2 on the leftwing and O3 on the right wing. Both wing men move towards the basket looking for a pass. If a pass is not made, O3 sets an outside-lateral-screen for O2, who crosses the three-second lane, cuts off O3's screen and moves into a sidecourt shooting position. As this action is taking place, trailer O4 cuts to the basket to the left-wing position vacated by O2. Often this area is

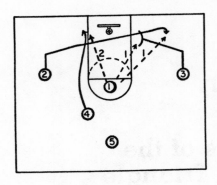 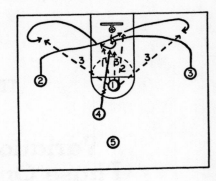

Diagram 11-1   **Diagram 11-2**

clear as the defensive man in that area follows O2 across the lane. You can see the numerous shot possibilities shown in the diagram. Also, O1 is always a threat to shoot and should feel free to do so, especially since teammates are moving into good rebounding positions.

The next maneuver is the Cross-over (Diagram 11-2). In this maneuver, both wing men cross over to the opposite side of the lane (if there are no shooting opportunities available on their side of the basket). When O2 and O3 begin crossing, the player on the right, wing man O3, sets a screen for O2 in front of the basket. Player O2 cuts off the screen in the direction of the ball. Screener O3 moves in the opposite direction. If neither player receives a pass, both players should move along the baseline on opposite sides of the lane to form an open triangle. While this action is taking place, O4, the trailer, executes a change of pace, then races to the basket. The shot possibilities are displayed in the diagram indicated in this paragraph.

The next two diagrams indicate plays off the Lopsided-triangle. This triangle is formed when the ball handler dribbles to either side of the free throw circle to an area right or left of the free throw line. This maneuver opens up the weakside wing area for a cutter and the free throw area for a jump shot. This play is shown in Diagram 11-3. Player O1 dribbles to the right side of the free throw circle. Player O2 is the right wing man moving towards the basket. Meanwhile, O3 cuts to the basket from the left-wing position on the weak side to receive a pass for a lay-up shot. Trailer O4 moves up the center of the court to the free throw line for a possible pass and jump shot. Player O5 remains in the safety position.

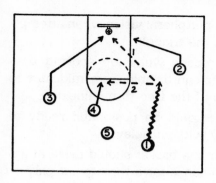 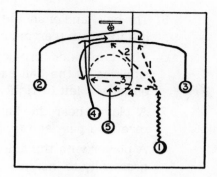

Diagram 11-3   **Diagram 11-4**

A second maneuver off the Lopsided break involves cutting and screening, as shown in Diagram 11-4. The following action takes place: O1 has the ball on the right side point-position. Right wing man O3 and left wing man O2 make their breaks toward the basket, then continue crossing the three second lane to the opposite sides. Player O2 stops immediately outside the lane on the right. Meanwhile, trailer O4 sets a down-screen on the left side and outside the three second lane for O3. Player O3 uses the screen to move along the outside of the lane looking for a pass. If O3 doesn't receive a pass, O3 stops at the free throw line extended. Player O4 breaks toward the basket for a pass. If O4 does not receive a pass, O4 quickly moves out to the right side of the lane. The safety-man O5 moves in the area midway between the free throw line and the circle to assume a shooting position.

Even with all of this maneuvering (which should take five seconds or less after ball possession), the Phase two delayed break should be utilized.

COACHING POINTS

1. The coach should designate the triangles and the maneuvers to be used during each game.
2. If possible, the ball handler should continue dribbling until ready to make a pass.
3. The ball handler should be ready to shoot when a good shot is available.
4. The power lay-up is an ideal shot for a player moving into a congested area under the basket.

5. The ball handler should use peripheral vision when attempting to locate teammates in the triangle.

6. The Lop-sided break increases weakside scoring possibilities as the ball handler can dribble from midcourt to either the left or right side of the free throw line.

7. A player near the basket should be positioned ready to receive a pass and to shoot without delay.

8. A player with the ball near the basket should drive in aggressively to increase the chance for a three-point play.

TIP 12

The Release-Man Fast Break

OVERVIEW

The fastest method of moving the ball up-court on a Phase one fast break (Tip 10) is passing. In order to attempt to score in the five seconds after the rebounder secures the ball, two things must take place. First, the rebounder must release the ball to a teammate at least twenty feet from the defensive basket (away from the area congested with players). Second, the ball must be passed up-court to the top of the free circle in the offensive frontcourt as quickly as possible. This will give the offensive team a chance to outnumber the defensive players for an easy basket via a dribble or a pass.

The Release-man fast break helps accomplish this task. By releasing a player immediately after the opponent's attempted shot, the player should be in position to receive a deep pass in the offensive court. To accomplish this, the player releasing races up the center of the court to the free throw line, then moves to an area ten feet from the sideline along the free throw line extended on the side of the ball. The player moves back slowly toward the ball, looking to receive a pass. When receiving the ball, the release-man has the assignment of setting up the scoring thrust to the basket. The effectiveness of this type of fast break is dependent upon the ability of the release-man and the ability of his teammates to fill the triangle and trailer positions.

The defensive spot rebounding (Tip 9) makes it possible to release one player without significantly affecting the team's rebounding strength. Often, after an opponent scores a basket, an alert offensive player can take the ball out of the net and inbound it to an outlet man, who may relay a long pass to the release-man for an easy score. This quick type of basket can be most demoralizing to a team that has just scored.

EXECUTION

It is better to designate a player to be the release-man in order not to confuse the other four teammates. The four should be able to rebound as well as five players if they position themselves correctly. In addition, with a man releasing up-court, at least one defensive player will probably follow him, making it a 4-on-4 rebounding situation. The shooting by an opponent guarding the release-man can very well be affected by changing his shooting rhythm to a more hurried type of shot. An added feature is to have the outlet man receiving the pass race-dribble the ball to the free throw line as quickly as possible if he cannot get the ball to the release-man.

Diagram 12-1 shows the rebounding setup and the assignment of the release man, in addition to the method used in moving the ball up-court. In the diagram, players O3, O4, and O5 occupy the rebound positions near the basket. Player O2 should take the rebounding position at the free throw line. After the rebound, O2 should move to the right wing position. After O5 rebounds the ball, it is passed to O2, in the right outlet position on the ball side. (An

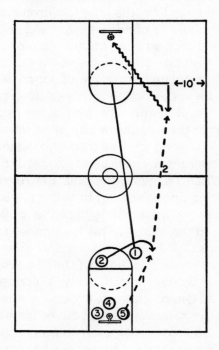

Diagram 12-1

outlet man should go to the ball side or middle area at least twenty
feet away from the opponent's basket.) Meanwhile, O1 has released
immediately after the shot, races up the middle of the court, makes
a 90 degree turn at free throw line extended, and goes to the side of
the outlet man. If the ball is released to the middle area, then the
release-man O1 can go to either side of the court. **Player O1 should
not stay in the middle court area.** Moving to a sideline makes it less
difficult for a player to secure an uncontested pass. The defensive
players are reluctant to attempt an interception or even to contest a
pass for fear of leaving the center court open for a scoring opportunity.

In Diagram 12-1, O2 passes to release-man O1. The release-
man has the option to drive to the basket, drive to the free throw
line, pass to a cutter going to the basket in the middle-court or
passing it to a player at the free throw line. In this diagram, O1
drives to the basket for a lay-up shot.

Diagram 12-2 is a sample of how quickly a team can score if the
defensive player is drawn out of position by following the release-
man. Player O5 rebounds and dribbles to the right side, moving

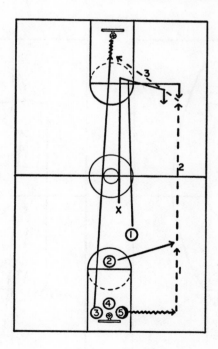

Diagram 12-2

away from a more congested area. O5 passes to the short outlet O2 also on the right side. Player O2 passes to release-man O1, who executes the proper basic movement for a player occupying this position. Player O1 starts to double back towards O2 to receive the ball. Player O1's defensive opponent follows O1, leaving the middle-court area unguarded. Player O1 receives the pass, then passes to O3, who is racing up the middle of the court by himself for a drive toward the basket for an attempted lay-up.

A typical complete fast break play is shown in Diagram 12-3. The play begins with O3 receiving the rebound on the left side. O3 passes to outlet man O2, who throws the long pass to release-man O1. Player O1 in turn passes it to O5 near the free throw line. Player O1 then assumes the left-wing position on the fast break. Meanwhile, O4 races to fill the right-wing position and O2 assumes the trailer role. Rebounder O3 becomes the safety-man, completing a Closed-triangle (Tip 10).

A similar play takes place after the ball is passed to the release-man (O1) in Diagram 12-4, except this time, O1 dribbles to

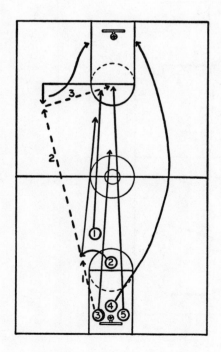

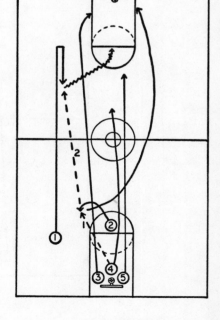

Diagram 12-3   **Diagram 12-4**

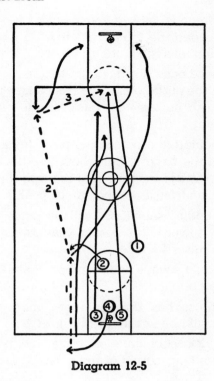

Diagram 12-5

the free throw line. The rest of the triangle positions are occupied by O2 on the right wing, O3 on the left wing, O5 is the trailer, and O4 is the safety-man.

The Release-man break can work very well after a basket also, as depicted in Diagram 12-5. Player O4 takes the ball out of the net and inbounds it to O2 on the left side. Player O2 passes to release-man O1, who in turn passes to O5 at the free throw line. O5 passes it to O2 taking the right wing position. Player O3 is in the trailer position and O4 is the safety-man. The release-man attack also works well after a made or missed free throw. If the short outlet player cannot make a long pass to the release-man, then he can begin to dribble the ball up the middle of the court. Usually the release-man's defender will move to protect against the drive by O2, making it possible to pass to the release-man. If not, the outlet man can dribble to the free throw line.

COACHING POINTS

1. The Release-man break works equally well off either the man-to-man or the zone defenses.

2. The outlet man is the key, inasmuch as he should assume a position beyond the top of the circle as quickly as possible after a teammate rebounds the ball.

3. The overhead pass is considered the best by the rebounder passing to the outlet man. The baseball or the chest pass is considered to be the best pass for the outlet man to the release-man.

4. Players should fill in respective positions in relation to distance from the basket. First should be the low position opposite the release-man, next is the free throw line, third is the trailer, and fourth is the safety position.

5. Good rebounding should be available since players are moving quickly towards the basket. Players should be ready to rebound a missed shot.

6. Players should always maintain body balance when passing or receiving a ball.

7. If the defense has three players back, then the Wide-triangle should be set up (Tip 10).

8. This is a quick score situation, not a wild, hectic attack. Five seconds is a long period of time. The Phase two break can also be used.

TIP 13

The Conversion of Interceptions, Recoveries, and Steals Into Quick Scoring Thrusts

OVERVIEW

Heavy emphasis should be placed upon converting quick scoring thrusts after recoveries (gaining possession of a loose ball), steals (taking a ball away from an offensive player), and interceptions. A high percentage of phase one fast break (Tip 10) baskets originate from these three types of turnovers. Consequently, there should be sufficient time spent developing fast break scoring thrusts after recoveries, steals and interceptions.

The important factors to consider in developing this part of the game are: (1) ball location, (2) number of players from both teams near the ball, (3) the flow of the offensive player movement, (4) the flow of the defensive player movement, and (5) the type of attack implemented by the offensive team. Each one of these factors is important because situations are set up necessitating various types of maneuvering to gain ball possession. This includes moving the ball to the basket, setting up a shot, and following up with a rebound if the shot is missed. There is also the possibility of the Phase two delayed fast break following the quick thrust, but the main focus of this tip is to score during the Phase one fast break—in other words, before the defense has been able to bring three or more players on defense to stop the fast break.

EXECUTION

Each player must be constantly aware of the factors mentioned earlier, especially in the fast-break game. The player gaining ball possession by a recovery, steal, or interception must envision the total scenario, then react quickly to his new role. Teammates must

69

also be aware of the new situation that might arise and react to their new roles.

The **action spot** is a term which refers to the location of the recovery, steal, or interception. The four players not involved in recovering the turnover must react to the actions that occurred in the action spot. With quick reaction, the players can create a rapid scoring thrust before more than two or three players can react defensively. The sequential order of the thrust should be: first, gaining possession of the ball; then, passing to a player moving towards the basket with a 2-on-1, 3-on-2, or 4-on-2; third, setting up a shot at the basket and then rebounding if necessary; and fourth, a retreating to a defensive position.

Dividing the court into areas is important in planning and execution of the fast break after turnovers. The closer the action spot is to the defensive team's basket, the greater the scoring opportunities. Rapid fire action is necessary to beat the opponents back on defense.

Diagram 13-1 depicts the division of the court by areas, plus

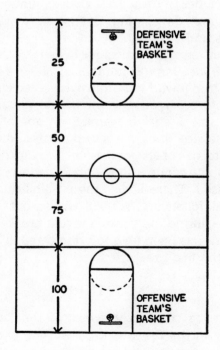

Diagram 13-1

the local time allotments for a scoring thrust from each area. The diagram shows the floor divided into four areas; number **100** is the area from the offensive team's basket to the top of the free throw circle. The number **75** area is from the top of the free throw circle to midcourt. From midcourt to the top of the free throw circle in the defensive backcourt is the number **50** area. Finally, the **25** area is from the top of the free throw circle to the offensive team's defensive basket.

A scoring thrust is geared to take two seconds from the **25** area, three seconds from the **50** area, four seconds from area number **75**, and five seconds from **100** area.

Diagrams 13-2, 13-3, 13-4, and 13-5 show examples of attacks from each area. In Diagram 13-2, the action spot is in the **25** area on the right side of the court. Player O1 is trapped by X2 and X3. Player O1 attempts a pass to O3 in the middle-court area. Player X4 intercepts the pass, then passes to X2 on the right side of the basket for a lay-up. Meanwhile, X4 and X3 follow in to assume rebounding positions. The other players should move toward the

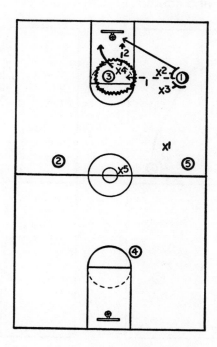

Diagram 13-2

action but are usually too far away to accomplish much on offense.

In another trap situation with the action spot in the **50** area (Diagram 13-3), the ensuing thrust takes place. Player O1 is trapped on the right side of the court and tries to pass to O2, in the middle court area. Player X1, guarding O2, intercepts the ball, creating the action spot. Player X1 passes to X5 on the left side, who in turn relays it to X2 breaking towards the basket from the right side for a lay-up. This was a 2-on-1 play. There are other methods to attack. For example, a 3-on-2 triangle could be formed by X5 dribbling to the free throw line and X1 along with X2 assuming the wing positions. Or, if X1 would dribble to the free throw line, then X5 and X2 would be the wing men.

In Diagram 13-4, O1 attempts a pass from a deep position in the right side backcourt to O4 at midcourt. Player X5 intercepts the ball, creating the action spot. Player X5 passes forward to X3 at the top of the free throw circle, who in turn passes to X4 on the weak-side wing position for a lay-up. Meanwhile, X3 and X2 follow for a possible rebound.

A common play is for the offensive player to dribble past a defensive player and attempt to maneuver the ball toward the bas-

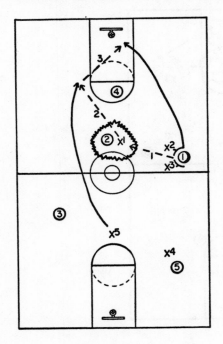

Diagram 13-3

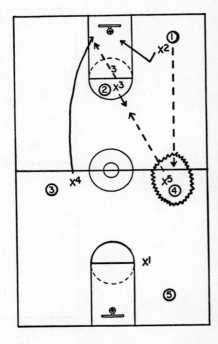

Diagram 13-4

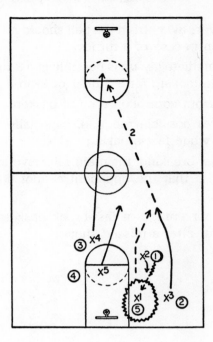

Diagram 13-5

ket. If the dribbler is delayed in the attempt by other defensive players sealing the path to the basket, the trailing, defensive player can catch up and deflect the ball from behind to a teammate. This is shown in Diagram 13-5. Player X2 slaps the ball away from O1 from behind and ahead to X1. From this action spot (in the **100** area), the other players quickly react moving up-court. Player X1 passes the ball to X3 on the right side of the court. Player X3 relays the ball up-court to X4 in the middle area. Player X4 goes in for a lay-up, while X5 and X3 are the potential rebounders. They also are in position to form a three-player triangle if needed.

COACHING POINTS

1. Practice setting up action spots and have players react both offensively and defensively.
2. When a player gains possession of the ball, he should endeavor to pass up-court to an open receiver closest to the basket as first choice, then to an open player up-court as a second choice.

3. The players away from the ball should be ready to make the transition in case of a turnover.

4. If no immediate lay-up is possible in a 2-on-1 situation, form a triangle looking for a 3-on-1 or 3-on-2 play.

5. Play fast but controlled type of basketball.

6. Look for a possible rebound, especially after a jump shot attempt when fast-breaking.

7. When fast-breaking, maintain offensive and defensive floor balance so that the opponent cannot score a quick, easy basket.

8. A high percentage of fast-break baskets are scored by a rebounder after a missed shot.

TIP 14

Change Roles for
A Better Numbers Fast Break

OVERVIEW

Fast-breaking by the numbers is probably the simplest way to teach the fast attack. We use the numbers fast break early in the season and occasionally later on as a change of pace to our more diversified break.

The numbers fast break means giving each player a number and assigning that numbered player a role and a spot on the Transition phase one fast break (Tip 10). The reason for assigning players to specific roles and positions on the break is related to logical assignments to utilize a player's abilities. Each player knows his assignment and role and races to carry them out.

The Phase two delayed break may be added if you desire, since the triangle is similar to the triangle in a regular Phase one fast break.

EXECUTION

The basic player assignments of the number fast break should be explained first, then the discussion will focus on a method to change numbers and roles. The players are given the following number, role, and position on the break:

- **Number 1:** This is the best ball handler. Player 1 must receive the ball as quickly as possible beyond the top of the defensive free throw circle. From there, this player dribbles at top speed up-court to the free throw line near the offensive basket. Player 1 may pass to any player in scoring position at any time.

- **Number 2:** Is the other backcourt player. Player 2's role is to move quickly up-court to the left-wing position for a long or short pass leading to a lay-up. If he doesn't receive a pass, 2's spot is on the left side of the basket, immediately outside the block. Player 2 may also flare out away from the basket.

- **Number 3:** Is the best outside shooter among the frontcourt players. Player 3's role is to race up-court for a position on the right side baseline about sixteen to eighteen feet from the basket. Player 3 is permitted to shoot whenever an opportunity presents itself.

- **Number 4:** Is the fastest and most versatile frontcourt player with a good assortment of shots. Player 4's role is to move directly toward the basket, then occupy the low-post on the right side. Player 4 may move to the left low-post in order to follow the ball. Scoring inside is 4's main role.

- **Number 5:** Is the slowest frontcourt player, and has the responsibility of being a safety-man. Because he is positioned at the top of the circle behind player 1, he should then move toward a free throw line—free throw circle spot for a possible jump shot.

Diagram 14-1 shows the basic numbers fast break position alignment near the offensive basket. Player O1 is the ball handler at the free throw line; player O2 is on the left side of the basket. (The

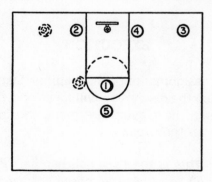

Diagram 14-1

dotted O2 is the flare-out position.) Player O3 is the shooter stationed in the right baseline area. Player O4 is at the low-post and on the right side. Player O5 is in the safety-man position; the dotted circle is O5's inside jump-shooting offensive position.

Diagram 14-2 depicts a typical fast break after a defensive rebound (assuming that zone or spot rebounding, Tip 9, was in effect). Player O3, the ball possessor, passes to O1 on the left side, beyond the top of the free throw circle. (The ball could have been passed to O2, but O2 would have to pass it to O1 as quickly as possible.) O1 dribbles up-court as quickly as possible to the free throw line. (Player O1 may zig-zag to avoid defensive players, rather than pass to another teammate, unless the pass leads to a direct scoring play.) Player O2 crosses over to the left side of the lane to occupy his position. Player O4 races up the middle of the court to the basket, then takes the right low-post. Player O5 moves to the safety position (the players are numbered according to roles and positions for clarity).

Diagram 14-3 shows another typical numbers fast break which takes place after a basket. Player O5 inbounds to O1, who dribbles it

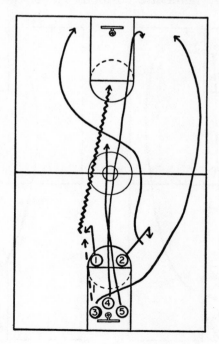

Diagram 14-2

up-court rapidly. The other players fill in the proper positions. (O5 could inbound from either side of the basket.)

Often players are in poor position to react or to race to the proper position. A good ball handler may be defensed so well that valuable time would be lost trying to pass him the ball. The logical move, then, would be to automatically change numbers for that ball possession. The rule we use is that whenever the change system is utilized, the guards may interchange rules on any possession. However, the big players move to offensive positions 3, 4, and 5 in that order, related to whether they are the third, fourth, or fifth player over the midcourt line. These simple changes confuse the defense. It may seem that a player may not be in a position compatible with his abilities. But as a change of pace, this makes little difference since the fast break is a quick strike attack, followed by the offense pattern.

Diagram 14-4 shows an example of the change. Player O5 rebounds the ball and passes to O2, who speed-dribbles to the free throw line (number 1 position). Player O1 sprints up-court to the left side of the basket (number 2 position). Player O5 races to the bas-

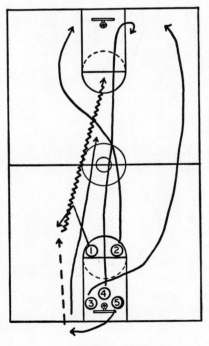

Diagram 14-3

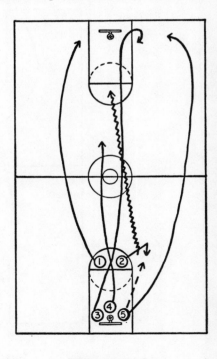

Diagram 14-4

ket, then to the right baseline area (number 3 position), and player O3 moves quickly to the basket, then to the right low-post (number 4 position). Player O4 takes the safety position (number 5 position), completing the change of all five players' roles.

Most of the time, only two or three changes need to take place.

COACHING POINTS

1. The dribbler should race up-court following any possession. This speedy tactic puts pressure on the defense.

2. The positions at the basket area should be occupied in less than five seconds, following a rebound or after an opponent's basket.

3. Two-on-one quick strike fast breaks may be tried whenever possible.

4. Any advantageous quick scoring thrusts before the positions are occupied is permissible.

5. Use the numbers fast break without stopping for ten minutes as a conditioning drill in practices.

6. Excellent rebounding is possible because players are moving fast to the basket, plus operating offensively in good rebounding positions.

7. Player O5 may crash the boards on shots with player O3 going back on defense. Player O2 may also go back on defense if he doesn't have an inside rebounding position.

8. A numbers fast break can originate equally well from both man-to-man and zone defenses.

TIP 15

Defending the Transition
Break Chronologically

OVERVIEW

The transition break is used by most teams. It is an invaluable weapon in any team's offensive arsenal. The quick scoring transition break forces the opponent to develop and execute another phase of defense successfully in order to win the game.

Your defense should be set up systematically in order to contain the transition break—from the inception on the Phase one fast break through the completion of Phase two delayed fast break. There are three vital objectives in defensing the transition break. They are: (1) prevent the outlet pass that initiates the fast break, (2) delay the progress of the ball, and (3) defend against the offensive tactics used near the offensive team's basket. The three defensive objectives serve to buy time to allow defensive players to retreat so that they can deny the easy field goal.

There are five steps necessary to attain the three defensive objectives. The first is to **seal** the rebounder gaining possession of the ball. (**Seal** means to contain his movement and to prevent him from making a quick outlet pass.) The second is to seal or defense the player receiving the outlet pass. This player should be controlled by forcing him to dribble to the sideline on the player's side of the court. The third step is for the other players to quickly retreat to a drop-back, 2-2 box zone to protect the basket area, while the fifth man contains the ball handler and thereby delays that player's efforts to continue dribbling the ball up-court. The fourth step is to switch to a 2-1-2 drop-back zone in order to stop both Phase one and Phase two attacks. The fifth step is to shift to the assigned drop-back defense, if possible, to counter any offensive action on the part of the opponents.

All five steps can be used to defend against the transition game after made or missed field goals or free throws. However, steps two, three, four, and five should be used when the break originates from a recovery, a steal, or a pass interception. Finally, steps four and five may be used whenever it is not possible to use one, two, and three.

EXECUTION

Essentially, the speed of the defensive players in carrying out their roles is extremely important. Often, even if a player is out of position in defensing the break, he can re-position himself with speed without affecting the team defense.

Diagrams 15-1 through 15-4 show sequential progression on defensing the transition break.

In Diagram 15-1, O5 has possession after rebounding a missed shot. (Both teams are still in rebounding positions.) The team on

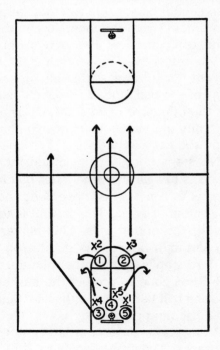

Diagram 15-1

offense moves to set up a fast break with O1 and O2 occupying the outlet positions. Players O3 and O4 should then move up-court. For the defensive team, X1 should seal ball handler O5. Players X2 and X3 should move back to their defensive basket area. Meanwhile X5 and X4 take defensive positions to the left and right side of the free throw circle respectively, looking to intercept a pass intended for outlet players O1 or O2.

Following the action in Diagram 15-2, let's assume the ball has been successfully passed to outlet player O2. Player X5 should seal O2 if possible; if not, X5 defenses O2 when O2 begins to dribble up-court by forcing O2 to the sideline area, as indicated in the diagram. While this takes place, X5's teammates have retreated to a 2-2 box defense near the defensive basket (indicated by dotted lines). Players X2 and X3 are side by side inside the free throw area, while X1 and X4 line up side by side near the top of the free throw circle. Also shown in the diagram is O2 passing to O1 in the middle court area, to continue the fast break (otherwise, the break would be forced to terminate). This leads to the defensive action shown in Diagram 15-3.

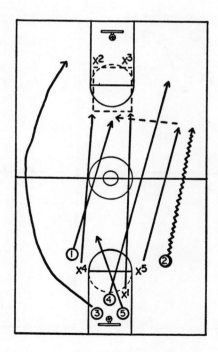

Diagram 15-2

In Diagram 15-3, ball handler O1 is near the free throw line (after O1 receives a pass from O2). Player O3 on the left side and O4 on the right side of the basket set up a Triangle-and-one with O2 occupying the right baseline-sideline corner. Player O5 takes the safety-man spot. To defense this alignment, X1, X2, X3, and X4 remain in their 2-2 zone box (which is part of the 2-1-2 zone). Player X1 guards O1 with X4's help. Meanwhile, X5 races to the corner to guard O2, when O2 receives a pass from O1.

There are other rotations possible once the box is set up; for example, X1 could cover O2 and X5 could replace X1. Or if X3 should cover the corner, X1 would drop back to occupy the vacated position and X5 would replace X1.

With the ball in the right corner in O2's possession, the 2-1-2 zone is now fully set up. Defensive protection develops from the 2-3 zone's Flattened-out corner alignment (Tip 2).

Diagram 15-4 shows this alignment, plus defensive movement to follow a pass to a perimeter player. Player X5 covers ball handler O2 in the right corner, while X3 and X4 help form the three-in-line back row near the baseline and X1 and X2 form the two players in

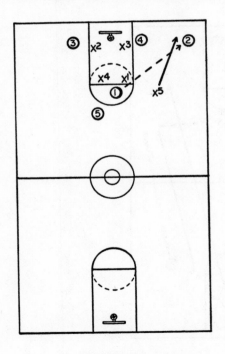

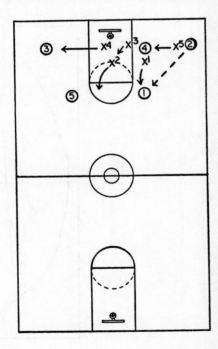

Diagram 15-3   Diagram 15-4

the front line row (Flattened-out 2-3 zone). On the next pass to O1, X1 guards O1, while X1's teammates fill in the rest of the 2-1-2 zone positions with the ball near the top of the free throw circle.

The 2-1-2 zone remains the basic drop-back defense until the Phase two delayed break threat terminates. If there is a two-to-three-second delay by the offensive team in starting their offensive pattern, the defense changes to the drop-back defense if it is different than the 2-1-2 zone.

COACHING POINTS

1. Defensing the transition break in chronological order takes a five player effort.

2. Sealing and delaying the ball from progressing up-court gives the defensive team more time to set their defense.

3. With the ball in the offensive backcourt, protect the basket area if there are only one or two players back on defense.

4. With the ball in the offensive backcourt, and with two players back on defense, the third player should defense the ball handler while the fourth and fifth players race back to the safety area.

5. Defensive players should race back to the safety area in straight lines.

6. Defensive players should get between the ball and the defensive basket as quickly as possible.

7. When rushing back to defend against the fast break, the defensive players should be ready to begin a fast break if a teammate recovers, steals, or intercepts the ball.

8. Once in the defensive area, the players should continue to be tenacious on defense. There is not any time to relax.

TIP 16

Beat the Man-to-Man Defense
With Weakside Scoring

OVERVIEW

Weakside scoring is important because it enables a team on offense to defeat a team using a sagging defense near the basket. Every offensive system should include the weakside attack. Although weakside plays to attack both man-to-man and zones are equally essential, the discussion here centers primarily on attacking the man-to-man defense. It is easier to locate an open weakside perimeter man against a zone defense, but more difficult to move inside.

It is possible to shoot from the perimeter or move in close to the basket against man-to-man: If certain maneuvers are executed properly, the task of defeating a man-to-man defense from the weakside is simplified. One should be aware that most man-to-man defenses are similar to zone coverage on and off the ball by incorporating the following guidelines. Play close to the ball handler, prevent an ensuing pass, sag to the middle from the weakside, drop back in order to be in line with the ball, switch players only when necessary, and force the ball toward the sidelines. There are many individual defensive moves and stunts, but they center around the basic guidelines just described.

An offensive pattern should be designed to beat the defense by combining many maneuvers to attack the center, the strong side, and the weakside. The offense can secure an inside position on a defense by taking outside shots when the defense sags. A balanced offense should be able to attack the middle, the strongside, or the weakside defense.

EXECUTION

It is easier to pass to the weakside when the ball handler is on either side of the free throw circle immediately above or below the free throw line and to either the left or right of the circle. It appears that there are more players available in key positions to receive passes without interceptions. For an example, the strongside post, the point-man, and the weakside wing should be in position for receptions.

The players on the weakside should be spread on the perimeter in order to be available for jump shots, drives to the basket, or quick passes to a teammate inside the shifting defense. Take advantage of a deep sagging defense by setting outside-lateral and down-screens to force the sagging players into a smaller defensive area, permitting short jump shots.

The ball may be passed from the strong side to the weakside by a direct pass, via a point-man, or by way of a post-man (on the side or in the three second lane) to a player on the weakside. The pass possibilities and a weakside play are shown in Diagram 16-1. The play originates from the right side with O1 possessing the ball. (The same type action can also be executed from the left side.) The offense pattern has three players on the strong side and two on the weak side. (Most patterns include this type of alignment.) The passing possibilities will be described first, followed by the description of the play. The three ways to move the ball from O1 to O4 are: (1) pass to perimeter player O2, who then passes to O4; (2) pass to post-man O5, who would pass to O4; or (3) a direct pass from O1 to O4. The passing lane most available at the time would dictate which pass play should be used.

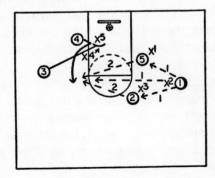

Diagram 16-1

On the weak side, O3 and O4 execute a Down-screen-reverse play. Player O3 sets a down-screen (Tip 6) for O4, who jabs-steps left, then moves to his right off the screen. The following important point should be emphasized—the more the strongside offensive players move after a pass to a weakside player, the less chance the sagging defense has to break up the play.

The defense in the diagram is standard by using the three basic defensive rules: (1) When guarding a player with the ball, play between the player and the basket as demonstrated in the diagram, X2 plays between O1 and the basket (Ball-You-Man rule); (2) The off-ball players play Ball-You-Man between the ball and their opponents; (3) The further each offensive weakside player is from the ball, the more a defensive player should sag off his man toward the basket area (Tip 2).

Now that the three ways of the passing to the weakside and the three defensive rules have been explained, the next four diagrams depict various offensive weakside plays. In Diagram 16-2, the Drive-sag-and-pass plays are shown. Player O1 has the ball in the strongside free throw line extended area. Player O2 cuts to the basket, then moves along the baseline to replace O3, who moved up toward O1. This maneuver tends to clear the free throw line area of some defensive strength. Player O1 drives toward the basket on the right side of the free throw lane until stopped by defender X2. However, this drive served the purpose of making the defensive players sag toward O1 to protect the basket. Player O1 passes to O4, who should be open along the weakside baseline, as the opponent X5 has sagged toward the middle. (This play is successful when O4 stays wide on the court.) Meanwhile, O5 is in the right low-post position. Player O5 could also move to the left low-post position for a pass from O4.

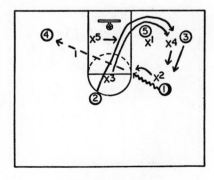

Diagram 16-2

Again with three players on the right side, ball handler O1 passes the ball to O2 to originate a play on the weakside. This play (note Diagram 16-3) is the weakside screen-and-roll play. Player O2 receives O1's pass, then from O2's left side of the circle position, O2 drives to the basket using an up-screen set by O4 to get free. Player O4 then moves toward the basket for a possible pass. Simultaneously, on the right baseline area O3 sets an outside-lateral screen on X1 to free O5 to move to a right-wing position.

The next two plays originate from a low post-man's pass. (This is possible from the post position on either side.) In Diagram 16-4, O1 passes the ball to low post-man O5. Players O1 and O3 then reverse for a possible return pass and shot. Player O2, who is left of the free throw circle, moves left, then veers sharply right. Meanwhile, weakside player O4 moves up to the free throw line and gets free by making a back-door cut to the basket for a pass and lay-up shot. Player O4 could set an up-screen for O2 as an alternate play.

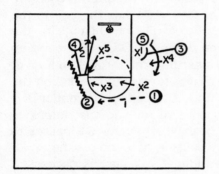

Diagram 16-3

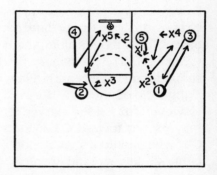

Diagram 16-4

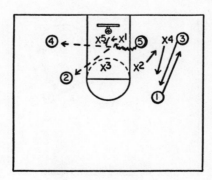

Diagram 16-5

In the second play, the low post-man drive is shown in Diagram 16-5. Post-man O5 makes a move toward the front of the basket to shoot or pass off to O2 on the left side of the free throw line, or to O4 on the left side of the basket. Players O1 and O3 reverse on the strongside to keep the defense honest.

COACHING POINTS

1. Perimeter weakside players should position near a passing lane, away from the basket ready to receive a pass and take a jump shot if in good shooting position.

2. A weakside offensive player should be ready to drive against an off-balance defensive player who is not in a good position to play defense.

3. Two weakside players should exchange positions after three or four seconds. Either player can set a screen for the other teammate.

4. A strongside ball handler should be aware of the action on the weak side.

5. The back-door play (Tip 11) should be used to keep the opponent honest, particularly if an opponent overshifts to the strongside carelessly.

6. The ball should be passed to a weakside player quickly in order to catch the defense out of position.

7. Inside rebounding position should be readily available to the offensive players, as defensive players, in attempting to secure the ball, have a momentary lapse, and thereby forget to secure a good rebounding position.

8. A weakside player near the basket should occasionally fake the jump shot to deceive an overanxious defensive player, then drive toward the basket.

TIP 17

Confuse the Opponent With the Automatic Twenty-Second Offense

OVERVIEW

Coaches looking for ways to embellish their offensive systems would do well to investigate the "Automatic Twenty-Second Offense." It offers a strong, deceptive, versatile, surprise set against the half-court man-to-man defense.

Three vital points:

1. It is an offense within an offense which, on a given cue, automatically goes into motion.
2. It is a totally organized offense composed of six sequential steps designed to produce the close-range shot or baby jumper (twelve-foot shot).
3. The entire attack, with all its screens and maneuvers, can be executed within twenty seconds.

Remember, the Twenty-second offense is a distinct entity, not an option. That means it can originate any time within the 1-3-1 attack, the 3-2 open key, the passing (motion) game, the 1-4 stack, the 2-3 low-post, etc.

Advantages of the Automatic
Twenty-Second Offense

1. It may be used as an alternative offense whenever a team is having a problem with any phase of its regular offense; and is particularly useful to relieve defensive pressure that is slowing down ball movement.

2. It has four players racing for the basket, with various cuts and screens available to free them for both passes and shots.

3. It is designed to get inside the defense or to jam the defenses inside the three-second lane for short jump shots.

4. It has sequential order that finds the center winding up at the low-post for a 1-on-1 move or a close-range hook or jump shot.

5. It offers good rebounding and defensive positioning.

It can be used often or sparingly during a game. If it doesn't produce a shot within twenty seconds, the team can go back to its original offense.

EXECUTION

The offense is keyed by the pivot-man (or other designated player) suddenly moving out to a point about three feet above the circle with his hands in an upward position. As soon as the pivot-man receives the ball, the offense is started.

The Automatic Twenty-Second Offense is effected in a six-step progression:

- **Step 1:** The pivot-man O5 moves out to the top of the circle with his hands raised upward.

- **Step 2:** As soon as O5 receives the ball, the two deepest players on opposite sides of the court cross under the basket, screening in order to be available for a pass ("mix-up play"). (Check players O3 and O4 in Diagram 17-1.) Meanwhile, the two players farthest from the basket break for the blocks along the three-second lane, ready to set or take advantage of a screen. (Check players O1 and O2 in Diagram 17-1.)

- **Step 3:** If no shot is available to a player by the mix-up play, O4 and O3 should move out of the three-second lane and into the wing areas within fifteen feet of the hoop as displayed in Diagram 17-2.

- **Step 4:** If before or after a pass to the player on the wing, and if a shot is not attempted, the two players in the low-posts (O1 and O2) should quickly move to the corners to form a three-back and two-front alignment with the middle area open.

- **Step 5:** If the triggerman at the top passes to either wing man, the triggerman should cut to the basket for a return pass. If the pass is not made, he should post up low on the ball side of the court (Diagram 17-4).

- **Step 6:** If the ball is passed to a player in a corner and a shot or pass is not taken, the center can set a screen for a give-and-go play.

If all of this sequential action fails to produce a shooting opportunity, the ball is passed or dribbled out to the point where the team should reset for its regular offense.

One other general rule is in effect at all times: Whenever the strong side is attempting to position for a shot at the basket, the weakside players should be screen-reversing. Rule of thumb: when closer to the basket than fifteen feet, use a down-screen; when fifteen feet or more away, use an up-screen.

In taking a closer look at the actual workings of the offense, observe Diagram 17-1: O5 has moved up to the top of the circle for the pass that will trigger the beginning of play. Players O3 and O4,

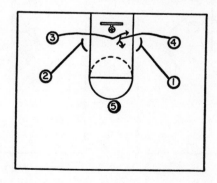

Diagram 17-1

being nearest to the basket on opposite sides, cut across the lane looking for a pass and easy shot.

Meanwhile, O1 and O2, being farthest from the basket, move to their lane block to set a lateral or down-screen. In this instance, they should set outside-lateral screens for O3 and O4.

Diagram 17-2 shows O1 and O2 setting up outside-lateral screens for short jump shots by O4 and O3 on the wings. Players O1 and O2 should maintain the low-post positions for possible inside shots. Any of the four players can receive a pass if open. If a shot does not occur within three seconds, O1 and O2 should usually go to the corners to help set up the three-back two-front alignment with the middle open referred to in Step 4.

If the situation is right, however, O2 and O3 can run a variation called the Reverse play (Diagram 17-3). Player O3 moves by the up-screen set by O1, while O2 maneuvers to the wing near O4's down-screen. The open player receives the ball. Key point: Player O5 may choose to dribble and drive toward the basket or dribble closer for a jump shot.

Diagram 17-4 assuming that the team has not scored and the players have moved to the proper positions on the court, O5 then passes to O2 and breaks sharply toward the basket (center cut). If the pass is not forthcoming, O5 occupies the low-post on the ball side. Meanwhile, O1 down-screens for O3 who reverses to replace O5.

Diagram 17-5: O2 passes to O5 and then down-screens for O4, who jab-fakes and takes advantage of the screen. On the weak side, O1 up-screens for O3, who in turn cuts for the basket.

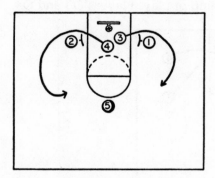

Diagram 17-2

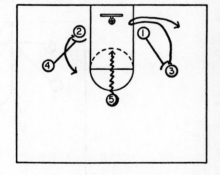

Diagram 17-3

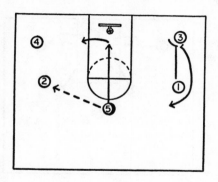

Diagram 17-4

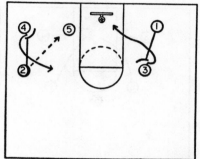

Diagram 17-5

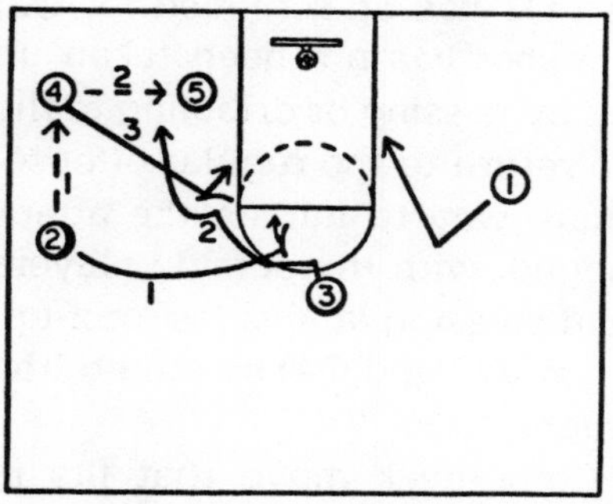

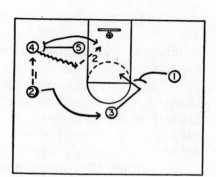

Diagram 17-6

Diagram 17-7

Diagram 17-6 shows what should take place when the ball is passed to the cornerman O4 and then into the pivot-man O5. This movement is called the Head-hunt. After passing, O2 goes the opposite direction to screen for O3, while O4, after passing to O5, moves toward the foul line extended to reinforce the screen on O3's opponent. This consecutive screening action serves to free O3 for a pass from O5, who should be in position to take a short jump shot. On the weak side, O1 fakes a reverse and goes toward the basket, looking for either a pass or a rebound.

Diagram 17-7 shows the final action of the automatic offensive sequence—the pick-and-roll between O4 and O5 from the corner. Pivot-man O5 moves to set an inside-lateral screen for O4, who drives for the basket. If O4 is prevented from completing the drive, he looks for O5 moving toward the basket. Meanwhile, O2 should

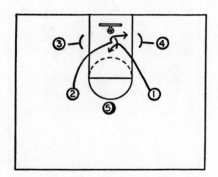

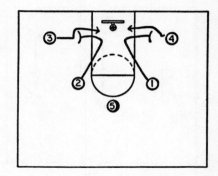

Diagram 17-8   Diagram 17-9

move to the top of the circle because O1 has up-screened for O3, who cuts over O1 to the basket. If a shot has not been taken up to this time, the ball should be cleared by passing or dribbling to the top of the circle area. This is a cue to return to the regular offense.

Diagram 17-8 depicts an alternate way to initiate the attack (Step 1). The order of cutting is changed, with the outside players O1 and O2 breaking for the basket and crossing lane sides (mix-up) play, and the players nearest the basket (O3 and O4) moving to the lane blocks to set outside-lateral screens.

Diagram 17-9 delineates the Come-back move that fits in nicely with either the standard initiation or the optional initiation. Cutters O1 and O2 move toward the basket, fake crossing, then come back to the same side to set inside-lateral screens for O3 and O4. To avoid confusion, O4 always cuts first. The mix-up can also be effective between O3 and O4, with O1 and O2 then becoming the wing men.

The success of the offense depends upon anticipation and recognition of the many scoring opportunities. The constant movement and the switching of screening assignments can create all sorts of problems for the defensive men and make them vulnerable to quick cuts for lay-ups.

COACHING POINTS

1. Every player should be ready to make a move or to shoot immediately upon receiving a pass. This is imperative because all of the offense occurs in the high percentage shooting area, where any delay can affect an excellent shooting opportunity.

2. Verbal cues may also be used to alert players to the offense. For example, a playmaking guard may call out a word or number as a sign for the pivot-man to move into position for the initial pass.

3. The initial receiver may be changed occasionally to avoid telegraphing the offense. Although the pivot-man is the usual choice, any front line player may assume the position at the top of the circle. This change should be indicated during a time-out or in a team huddle prior to the aligning for a free throw.

4. Players are given the liberty to change the directions and speed of their cuts or types of screens. Even the initial order of cuts and screens can be changed. This organized chaos can be very confusing to the opponents, which makes the offense even more effective.

5. Players should change roles from screeners to cutters spontaneously.

6. The continued movement helps move big defensive players away from the basket, weakening the internal defense and forcing them to play in an undesirable outside area.

7. Proper screening pressures the defense to execute many skills precisely (over the top, slide through, and switch), creating more opportunities for errors on the part of the defense.

8. The multi-movements make the offense difficult to scout and prepare against. Many opponents never realize it's a separate, highly organized attack.

TIP 18

Counter the Zone and Combination Defenses With the Figure Eight Offense

OVERVIEW

I spent the best ten minutes I have ever spent learning about basketball when Ted Kjolhede, the former outstanding basketball coach and current athletic director at Central Michigan University, explained his Figure eight offense to me. It is an offense used to combat the zone and combination defenses. I adopted the offense, added some variations, and found it to be an excellent weapon to counter both defenses.

The Figure eight has ball movement, player movement, inside plays, outside plays, weakside plays, and provides good rebounding positioning. There is opportunity for individual moves and provisions for utilizing abilities of the players. It is a relatively simple offense for coaches to teach and players to learn.

EXECUTION

The locations of players and their assignments will be analyzed first, then ball and player movement will be discussed. The initial pattern alignment is a 1-3-1. (Note Diagram 18-1.) The assignments are as follows: Point-man O1 plays at the top of the free throw circle, moving from one side to the other. Player O1 can pass to any open player or shoot. Player O1 should not go to the basket, nor should O1 reverse with a weakside player, unless assigned to do so as a special move. Pivot-man O5 plays a post position, generally remain-

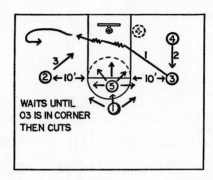

Diagram 18-1

ing in the high-post area. The two wing men, O2 and O3, position themselves at the free throw line extended approximately ten feet from the right or left side of the circle. The swing-man, O4, may start in either corner or at the low-post position.

The standard rules for attacking zones—driving the seams, passing sharply around the perimeter, using the point-player as a feeder, setting up a weakside player, creating a 1-on-1 drive by a player near the basket—should be used in conjunction with this attack. The player movement is relegated to the two wing men and the swing-man, moving in a Figure eight pattern (weave).

Diagram 18-1 shows the alignment and player movements. Player O3 cuts through the free throw lane near the basket. O4, from the right corner position, moves to replace O3. Note: O3 may change speed as he cuts through the lane. If a pass is not available, he may stop at the left low-post looking for a pass. If not, O3 continues to the left corner, and sets up for a pass. At this time, O2 duplicates O3's action except from the left wing by moving through the lane toward the right corner. Whenever a shot is attempted, O5 plus the wing cutter and the cornerman should rebound with the other wing man. The point-man should stay behind the free throw line for a high rebound or a defensive retreat.

Once the ball is passed to the post-man, all four players could conceivably be open to shoot. Passes initiated by the post-player are shown in Diagram 18-2. The action starts with a pass to the post-player O5 from right wing man O2. (Post-player O5 may pass to the weakside wing man O3 or to cornerman O4, back to right wing man O2, or to O1 near the top of the free throw circle.) Assuming there were not any shots taken, then the weave would take place with O3

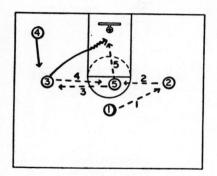

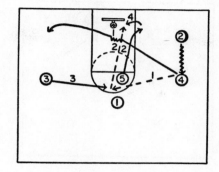

Diagram 18-2   **Diagram 18-3**

moving toward the basket, looking for a pass, and then relocating in the right corner. Player O4 should move to occupy the left-wing position. Player O2 should hold the right wing until O3 occupies the right corner, then O2 should make his cut. In the diagram, O5 receives a return pass from O3, then O5 passes to O3 cutting to the basket for a lay-up.

If a corner player has the ball and cannot shoot, he should simply dribble to the wing position on his side of the court, knowing that the weakside wing man will be cutting across the middle, then occupy the position O2 had vacated.

Diagram 18-3 illustrates a maneuver following a player dribbling out of a corner. Player O2, in the right corner with the ball, dribbles out to the open right wing position. Meanwhile, O5 breaks down to the right low-post. Cutter O3 moves from a wing position on the left side into the high-post position vacated by O5. (When a high post-man cuts to the basket, the weakside cutter goes opposite or to the high post. (Players should never move to the same position.) The post-man has the choice of breaking whenever he desires. The cutters should adjust to the post-man's maneuvers. Continuing with the play in the diagram, O2 passes to O3, cutting to the high-post position. Player O3 passes to low post-man O5. Meanwhile, O4 moves to replace the left wing man O3. (O3 should go to the right corner if he does not receive a pass from O2.) Again, O3 could conceivably pass to any of four teammates because they are all located in good shooting positions.

Diagram 18-4 shows a screen play immediately outside the three-second lane. Point-man O1 has the ball and passes to O2 on the left wing. Meanwhile, right wing man O3 cuts to the basket,

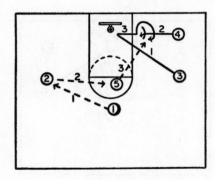

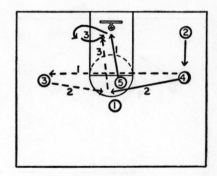

Diagram 18-4   **Diagram 18-5**

begins to cross the lane, then stops abruptly, changes directions, and moves parallel along the baseline toward the right side using the screen set by corner man O4 outside the right side of the lane to become free. Meanwhile, the ball is passed to high post-man O5, who passes it to O3 for the shot. Player O4 moves toward the basket for a possible pass. Notice that once again, all four players are in good shooting positions.

Another variation of the offense is shown in Diagram 18-5. This time the play starts with a crosscourt pass from strongside right wing man O4 to weakside wing man O3. (This pass is usually accessible.) Player O3 elects to pass the ball back to O4 moving into the high post position vacated by O5, who moved to the basket first, then to the low-post position on the left side. Player O4 passes to O5 for an attempted lay-up.

Diagram 18-6 is an example of how to alter the pattern by changing the cuts and cutters. This maneuver works well, but should be the exception rather than the rule. Player O1 passes to right wing man O4. Player O1 then cuts directly toward the basket from the point position to receive a return pass from O4 for a possible lay-up. While this takes place, O2 should move to occupy the point position and O3 should move to the left wing. If it is not possible to pass to O1, then the Figure eight weave should begin with O1 taking part in the movement while O2 stays at the point position. Other exchanges can take place but are not necessary.

As you can see, the imagination of the players can determine the potential number of plays which can be executed by using this offense.

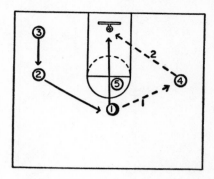

Diagram 18-6

COACHING POINTS

1. The wing man should cut when the cornerman is in position facing the basket.

2. The offense should attempt to move closer to the basket because the defense is being forced to retreat as the ball is being both dribbled and passed.

3. The point-man is a feeder but also should have many scoring opportunities by being aware of the zone shifts or sags in the middle area of the defense.

4. The cutters should always look for an opportunity to become free near the basket to shoot or to rebound prior to continuing on to the corner area.

5. The post-player should look for available cutting paths to the basket after passing to a wing man, a corner man, or a low-post man.

6. Players should read the defense to spot weaknesses and make clever cutting maneuvers to get free for a close-in shot.

7. A strongside wing man should pass the ball frequently to the weakside wing-man. This can be done via the perimeter, the post-man, or directly.

8. A wing man dribbling into a seam between two defensive players frees the point-man or wing man or cornerman for a shot. The point-man dribbling into a seam frees either or both wing men.

TIP 19

Attack the Zone Presses With Frontcourt Organization

OVERVIEW

The cardinal rule in attacking zone presses is to maneuver the ball to the basket in order to score as quickly as possible. Otherwise, the defensive team will probably have the advantage and therefore will gamble on the press and still have sufficient time to retreat to their drop-back defense. By being offensively orientated, a team should put pressure on the opponent by developing quick scoring thrusts. Repeated quick scoring thrusts can neutralize a zone press. A sophisticated, yet simple attack in the offensive frontcourt is essential to preventing defense from forcing turnovers and causing the offense to attempt bad shots.

The organized attack should include 2-on-1 situations which blend into 3-on-2 and 4-on-3 plays. This is made possible by a two-step attack. In the first step, once the ball is at midcourt it should be moved quickly in the close proximity of the basket. The second step is to use the Triangle-and-one pattern. The goal is to set up the shot and all important rebound positions (offensive rebounds account for many scores because first shots are often missed in the transition game).

EXECUTION

The frontcourt attack may be used in conjunction with any offensive press breaker. Zone press offenses are set up with one or two players stationed or moving close toward the basket, while the others assist in bringing the ball up-court. The ball usually can be brought to midcourt with a relatively high degree of success, but moving to the basket can be difficult because of the tactics used by retreating defensive players.

In the first step, from midcourt, a quick strike is attempted from one side of the court, from the middle, or from the weakside. Once the ball is moved close to the basket (second step), then the Fast-break-triangle and the Triangle-and-one should be implemented. However, 2-on-1 plays take precedence whenever they can be properly executed.

Both steps will be shown in Diagrams 19-1, 19-2, 19-3, and 19-4.

The attack in Diagram 19-1 is called the Dribble-and-set-up. The following action takes place: O1 has the ball a short distance from the front court on the left side. Player O5 is in a deep position on the left side high-post. The other players are well spread on the court. Ball handler O1 drives to the free throw line to set up a Closed-triangle with O5 on the left wing and O2 on the right wing. Player O4 fills the trailer position and O3 is the safety-man. All of the scoring maneuvers may be developed while forming and utilizing the triangle.

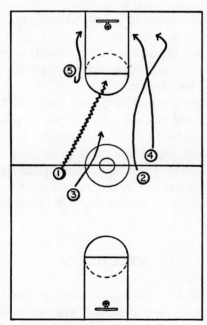

Diagram 19-1

The Center-hit-and-set (frontcourt attack) is shown in the next diagram (19-2). The following action takes place: O1 has the ball on the left side just near midcourt. Player O1 passes to O5 in the left high-post position, who pivots to face the basket looking for the two wing cutters. The two cutters are O1 on the left and O2 on the right. O4 fills the right trailer position on this Closed-triangle, and O3 is the safety-man. Again, there are multiple scoring opportunities available.

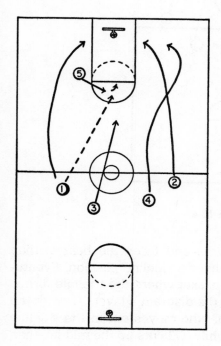

Diagram 19-2

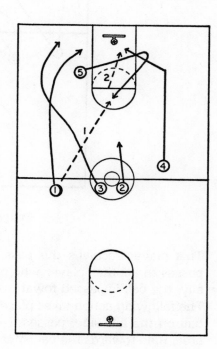

Diagram 19-3

In the third attack, the Weak-side-crash (back-door) (see Diagram 19-3), player O1 has the ball on the left side of the court. Player O5, in the deep position (left high-post), moves to the right side of the lane, then breaks to the high-post position to receive a pass from O1. Player O4 sprints for the basket on the weakside to receive a pass for a possible lay-up. If O4 does not receive a pass, then O1, on the left wing, and O3 the trailer, and O2 in the safety position, complete the Closed-triangle.

Finally, the Replacement attack (Diagram 19-4) is a method of bringing the ball along the sideline. The object is to pass to a player up-court as the player is moving back in the direction of the ball.

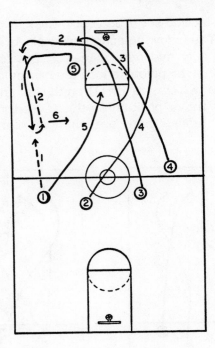

Diagram 19-4

This player receives the pass, turns and faces the basket, then passes to another player who occupies a sideline position. Eventually, the ball is passed toward the basket where the triangle forms. The following action takes place in the diagram. Player O1, with the ball on the left side, passes to O5, who moves out to the sideline area, then towards the ball. Meanwhile, O3 cuts up the middle, then veers left to the left sideline, then moves up to meet a pass thrown by O5. Player O4 goes to the left low-post while O1 fills the free throw line position, and O2 the right wing, and O5 becomes the safety-man. Again the Closed-triangle is established, and the pass may be made to any player open for a reception.

The step one movements may be combined to counteract defensive moves. For example, the attack can begin with the Replacement, switch to the dribble, and end up with a Weak-side-crash scoring play. Other combinations are possible when the players learn the step one movements and how they blend into a Triangle (step two).

COACHING POINTS

1. The four frontcourt attacks should also work against a man-to-man press.

2. After catching a pass, the player should pivot to face the basket, then pass or dribble toward the basket.

3. If the attack breaks down, look for a Phase two transition break play.

4. Even if the attack is disorganized in the back court, it is possible to set up a frontcourt attack (particularly the Weak-side crash and the Replacement).

5. The dribble can be a valuable method of moving the ball toward the basket.

6. The post-man should move towards the ball handler to receive a pass if he is closely guarded.

7. When a player is caught in a trap in the back court, he should make any successful pass possible; meanwhile his teammates should be ready to begin a frontcourt charge.

8. Remember, a high percentage of baskets are made by the offensive rebounding of missed shots, so practice follow-up rebounding often.

TIP 20

Setting Up a Star Player

OVERVIEW

What do you do with an outstanding player excelling in the offensive phase of basketball? How do you blend special abilities in with those of less talented teammates? When a coach finds a star, what should he do to take advantage of the exceptional player's offensive skill? Should the team's philosophy be to set up shots for a star the majority of the time? Should the star blend into the offense and let his ability shine through without special attention? Should all of the players execute the pattern while being constantly aware of the star's location, then give him the ball at an appropriate time to shoot?

I have observed that championship teams operate under the philosophy of teamwork; they use a balanced attack, yet find room for the skills of the exceptional offensive player.

Every championship team I have ever coached used the team concept and also used a gifted player as a decoy and feeder. This permitted other players to develop skills to carry a share of the scoring load by taking advantage of defensive weaknesses created when the opposition tried to use special defensive tactics to stop the star.

The following considerations are important in attempting to determine the star's special talents: (1) the size and endurance of the player; (2) his offensive skills; (3) the positions the star can play; (4) the ability of the opponents; and (5) how to combat and counter the defense or special tactics geared to prevent the star players from being most effective.

The team star referred to in this tip is a good ball handler possessing a high level of ability to pass, shoot, and play defense.

EXECUTION

The plays to be discussed are adaptable to any type of offense. They will be explained in relation to the type of player, by his position and by the team's offensive tactics. Also included are plays to attack the man-for-man and the zone defenses. (The combination defense should be attacked as if it were a zone.)

Attacking a Man-to-Man Defense

Screening for the star with and without the ball is essential to create scoring plays. The first play involves the star possessing the ball. This is the Dribble-and-roll continuity play, shown in Diagram 20-1. It involves spontaneous screen-and-roll plays helping the star (either a guard or a forward) work his way toward the basket. In the diagram, player O1 has the ball and drives off O5's screen to the right side of the free throw line. As is typical in screen plays, O5 screens and cuts toward the basket. Player O1 can move in for a shot, if possible, but O1 continues to dribble, looking for another screen-and-roll play. Player O4 sees the action and sets a screen on the right side of the lane near the basket. Player O1 drives left off O4's screen, while O4 rolls in to the right. Screens should be set closer to the basket each time. The Screen-and-roll continuity play makes the following options available: a drive to the basket for a stop and a jump shot, a fake drive and a shot, or pass to the player rolling toward the basket. Meanwhile, the other players reverse or keep moving, preventing their opponents from sagging in to stop the play, and can be open for a pass and shot.

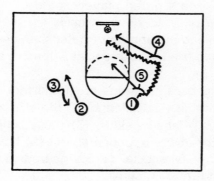

Diagram 20-1

The Pass-and-follow play shown in Diagram 20-2 is similar in theory to the Dribble-and-pass except that the star passes the ball instead of dribbling to create a screen-and-roll. To explain further, O1 passes to O2. Player O1 fakes a cut toward the lane and moves behind O2 for a return flip pass. Player O2 rolls toward the basket and then moves to the left side. Player O1 then passes to O3 along the free throw line to the right of the circle, fakes toward the basket, and goes behind O3 for a return pass. Player O3 accommodates O1, then moves toward the basket and then to the left side. When O1 sees that a play is not available, he passes to O5 at the right low-post position. Again O1 fakes a cut to the basket, then drops behind O5, who returns the ball to O1 and rolls toward the basket. Meanwhile, the players away from the ball move to open positions ready to receive a pass or to rebound. Note that there are shooting possibilities available to both the star and the screener in each screen play.

The theme in the next two diagrams is the multiple screens. They are designed to free a star player on either wing to shoot a short jump shot. In Diagram 20-3, O5 sets an inside-lateral-screen (Tip 6) for O1 on the right side. Player O1 cuts off the screen and crosses the lane near the left low post-man O4. Player O4 sets an Outside-lateral-screen, as does the left wing man O3. (This forms a double-screen.) Player O1 uses the double-screen in order to gain freedom to receive a pass from O2. Note that O2 dribbles to the free throw line, then passes to O3. This maneuver freezes the defense in a sag position permitting O1 to get free.

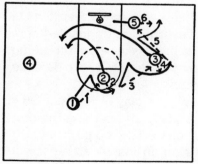

Diagram 20-2

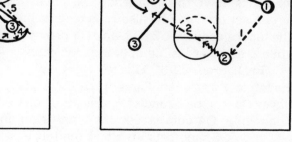

Diagram 20-3

The Cat-and-mouse play is described in Diagram 20-4. Again a star guard or forward is set up. The play is set up on the right side of the lane. Players O4 and O5 set a double-post facing the basket. Player O3, the star, stands next to O4 near the baseline facing O1, who has the ball at the top of the circle. Player O3 fakes left, then to the right repeatedly, looking to hook his opponent on screener O4. When this takes place, O3 moves either to the basket or to the right side for a pass and possible shot. Once O3 makes his move, O4 and O5 should roll in the opposite direction, with O4 staying low and O5 going high. Meanwhile, O1 and O2 reverse to keep the defense from sagging and also to try to get open.

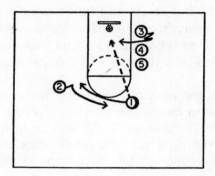

Diagram 20-4

If a star shoots well from the inside, move him to an offensive low-post position. Diagrams 20-5 and 20-6 show two ways to accomplish this. Player O1 has the ball on the right baseline area as star O5 is at the right low-post. Player O1 (who should be a good shooter) passes the ball to O5, who makes a move toward the basket. Meanwhile, on the weak side, O3 sets a down-screen for O4, then rolls down the lane while O4 moves right off an inside-lateral screen set by O2, who also rolls toward the basket after screening. The tactics used by O2, O3, and O4 prevent sagging by the defense, while creating possible openings for each.

In Diagram 20-6, O4 is the right low-post player, and star O5 is the left low post-man. Players O1, O2, and O3 are on the perimeter. Player O1, the ball handler, passes the ball to O2, who passes to O3. Meanwhile, O4 cuts across the lane using an inside-lateral-screen set up by O5, and sets up along the left baseline. Player O5 pivots and takes the low-post. Player O3 passes to O4, who in turn passes to O5. Player O5 drives to the basket to shoot or pass to another player.

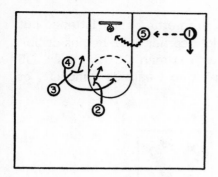

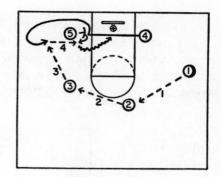

Diagram 20-5   **Diagram 20-6**

Attacking the Zone Defense

It is easier to set up a perimeter shooter against a zone than a man-to-man simply by passing the ball quickly to the weak side because the nature of the zone is to protect the inside. The following three diagrams show a play near the top of the circle against the 2-1-2 zone to the right side against the 1-3-1 alignment and the right baseline sideline against the Flattened-out 2-3 alignment (Tip 2).

In Diagram 20-7, O1 has the ball at the top of the free throw circle. The offensive team is playing the Figure-eight pattern (Tip 18). Player O1 drives the gap between X2 and X3, then passes to star O3 for a shot. (O1 could also pass to O4, or post-man O5; O3 could pass to the weak side cutter O2.)

In the Side court 1-3-1 alignment play (Diagram 20-8), O1 passes to O5 at a high-post position, who in turn passes to star player O3 on the weakside wing for the shot. (O3 could also pass to O4 in the corner or to O5 cutting to the left low-post.)

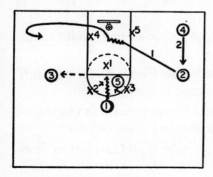

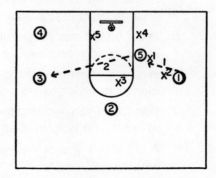

Diagram 20-7   **Diagram 20-8**

The objective in Diagram 20-9 is to attack the Flattened-out 3-2. Player O4, with the ball in the right corner area, begins dribbling to the wing, then passes to low post-man O5 (the star). O5 moves in to shoot. O5 could also pass to weakside wing O1, or weakside corner player O3.

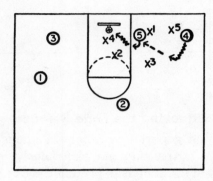

Diagram 20-9

COACHING POINTS

1. It is important for a star's teammates to be situated in shooting positions when a star has the ball.

2. Even though his teammates set him up, the star should be ready to shoot, drive, or pass, in that order, whenever receiving the ball.

3. A star jump shooter should perfect the jump pass to use when an opponent is in position to block the shot.

4. A star should master the jab-step fakes, change of pace, and change of direction footwork.

5. A tall inside star player should dominate a game with shooting, passing, and rebounding.

6. A star player should develop free throw shooting proficiency in order to take advantage of being fouled.

7. Use the Figure eight attack with the star guard in the weave to combat a box, or diamond and one zone defense.

8. A tall inside star or excellent jumper should be alert to score with the sky shot.

TIP 21

Using Three Designated Plays To Improve the Passing Game

OVERVIEW

The Passing game (motion offense) is an excellent offense against the man-to-man defense. Some coaches have tried to use this type of offense against a zone, but with little success.

The Passing game is designed with a few rules for both inside and perimeter players. Player movement, screens, and well-timed passes create scoring plays. The players are free to move in various directions at their discretion, making it difficult for the defensive players to guard their opponents and to determine which are the cutting lanes, passing lanes, and the players doing the screening.

There are three basic passing games. The Three game is a pattern with three perimeter men and two assigned post-men. The Four game includes four perimeter players with one assigned post-man. The Five game has all five players on the perimeter with any two players moving into any two post positions temporarily. The three game is the one which will be discussed. Here is a brief summary of the Three game rules for both perimeter and post-players.

The perimeter players without the ball can make the following moves: (1) cut to the basket, (2) screen a player away from the ball, (3) screen for the player with the ball, or (4) make a "V" cut (cut toward the basket then double back and occupy the same position). The perimeter player with the ball can pass the ball to any other player and then make the same moves. (Perimeter players may also set screens for any teammate making cuts.) Inside players set screens for each other or for cutting perimeter players. The screening process is the basis of this attack because it frees players for good opportunities to shoot. (Zone defenses minimize the screening potential, thus neutralizing the passing game.)

There are other rules, invented by ingenious coaches, which are related to player alignments (the true passing game does not need a formal alignment, only perimeter players and inside players), to spacing, and four types of screens: up, down, inside-lateral, or outside-lateral (Tip 6). All of the rules of the Passing game work well in the majority of the cases. However, the Passing game can also break down and fail to develop good shots.

There are three major problems which can cause a Passing game to falter. First, the team may be unable to repeat the same successful play consecutively. Second, it may be difficult to set up a player in a desirable offensive position, and third, players can keep moving and screening without creating any desirable offensive thrust.

These three weaknesses can be overcome by utilizing three plays. Each is a one-time attempt; it is then necessary to revert to the regular attack. The plays bring temporary formal structure to this free-wheeling attack.

EXECUTION

The three plays develop from the Three passing game (three perimeter and two assigned post players). The ball handler can give a verbal signal, a hand signal, or an individual movement signal, such as a stutter dribble to initiate one of the plays.

The Clear-out-drive is the first play (Diagram 21-1). Player O1 passes to O2, who passes immediately back to O1. This is the signal that the Clear-out-drive play is to take place. (This play always originates from the top of the free throw circle.) Player O2 then sets an inside-lateral-screen on O1's opponent. Player O1 drives to left (always opposite his positioning at the top of the free throw circle, which in this case is the right side) down the lane to the basket. Meanwhile, O4 on the right low-post moves up the side of the lane to the free throw line. Left low post-man O5 clears to the right side, halfway up the lane. Player O3 also clears to the right side. Players O3 and O5 should be ready to rebound the shot.

The second play is the back-door play by the two post-men (Diagram 21-2). The ensuing action takes place with both post-men playing low, while the other three players are spread along the

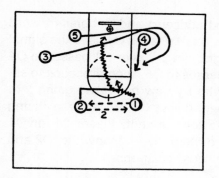 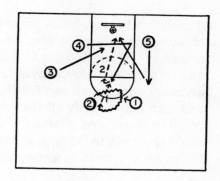

Diagram 21-1   **Diagram 21-2**

perimeter. Player O2, the ball handler, begins dribbling toward O1 from left of the free throw circle to the right side. Just as it appears he is going to pass to O1, player O2 makes a spin-dribble and drives toward the left side. This is the signal for initiating the play. Player O4 moves from a left low-post position to the right side as though he were planning to set an inside-lateral-screen for O5. Then O4 races up to the free throw line to receive a pass from O2. Player O5 fakes using O4's non-existent screen, then moves quickly into the right wing position. Just as O4 receives the pass from O2, O5 makes a back-door cut to the basket for a pass from O4 and a possible lay-up shot. Player O3 then moves into rebounding position.

The third play is the Wing's block screen play (Diagram 21-3). The players are in the following positions: O5 (high-post), O4 (low-post), and O1 (the ball handler) near the top of the circle, while O2 and O3 are on the left side of the court. Player O1 starts the play

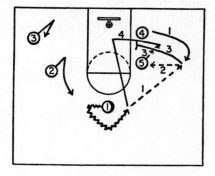

Diagram 21-3

dribbling left, then backs up toward midcourt and dribbles forward in a triangle (this is the play three signal). Player O4 sees the signal and reacts by moving out to the right wing. Player O1 passes to O4 and cuts to the basket. Player O4 passes to O5, then proceeds to set an outside-lateral-screen for O1, who by now has faked going left, and then cuts sharply off O4's screen. Player O1 proceeds to a wing position to receive a pass from O5 for the shot. Player O5 or O1 could also pass to O4 cutting toward the basket. Meanwhile, O2 and O3 make V-cuts to reoccupy their same positions.

COACHING POINTS

1. There is usually time for each play to develop regardless of the player's location.

2. A play can be initiated anytime the offense is sputtering.

3. Do not force a play into the attack when it is not needed.

4. A coach can designate the play and the players to be involved during a time-out.

5. Techniques such as a jab-step, a head and shoulder fake, or a faked pass assists the execution of offensive plays.

6. Players should stay away from a teammate driving in the direction of the basket.

7. When a player drives along the side of the lane, a teammate should set a screen or clear out by going to the other side of the court.

8. The Automatic twenty-second man offense (Tip 17) may also be used when players are experiencing difficulty in setting up a shot.

TIP 22

Capitalizing on a
Fronted Post-Man

OVERVIEW

Hitting a team in the middle of their defense by scoring inside and under the basket can force the opponent to be somewhat demoralized. When this takes place, the defensive players tend to become upset and lose confidence. A defense cannot hold up successfully when an offense is able to penetrate the internal area and score consistently.

Both man-to-man and zone defenses use the Ball-You-Man principles (Tip 2) anywhere on the court, including guarding any post-man. Ideally, the defensive man guarding a low-post player attempts to front the opponent while the standard play is to guard a high-post player from a side position with a hand in a position extended toward the front of the opponent to discourage or deflect passes.

The objective of the pivot-man is to prevent the defensive player from fronting him or from intercepting a pass when the post player establishes an inside position on the defensive player. To do this, the player in the post position (the regular post-man or any other player "posting") must be quick, strong, and clever to maintain a position to receive a pass. Lob passes over the defensive player when fronted and passes away from the defensive player are the most successful. The objective in this tip is to take advantage of a fronted post-man.

EXECUTION

The passer and receiver must coordinate their efforts with good timing and good positioning to make a play work properly. The first

123

three diagrams (22-1, 22-2, and 22-3) will show how to pass the ball
to a fronted post-man against the man-to-man defense while the last
three diagrams (22-4, 22-5, and 22-6) will feature the post-man
receiving a pass against a zone.

Pivot-Man With Inside Position
Scoring Against a Man-to-Man Defense

Whenever a post-man is fronted, the easiest method for him to
score is to receive a lob pass over the defensive player. This can
take place quite often when the offensive player occupies a low-post
position (as the low-post player is usually fronted in most defenses).
This is the most effective method. The post-man with inside position
holds this position until a teammate can give him a lead-lob pass.
The other offensive players must draw their defensive players away
from the weak side of the court, thereby eliminating weakside defensive help.

Diagram 22-1 shows the lob pass without any defensive weakside help. Player O1 in the corner has the ball and passes to O2 near
the baseline-sideline area. X1 fronts low post-man O5. Notice that
O4, the weakside player, is stationed above the left side of the free
throw line. This enforces the Clear-out-the-weakside-help concept.
This maneuver and the one that follows can be part of any offensive
pattern. In the play, O2 lob passes to O5, who has inside position,
for a possible lay-up shot.

Diagram 22-2 shows a similar alignment except that weakside
man O4 is in the left-wing position. This time O1 passes to O3, who

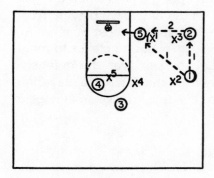

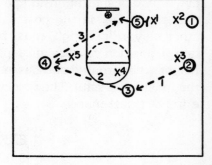

Diagram 22-1   **Diagram 22-2**

in turn passes to O4. Then O4 (guarded closely by X5) passes to post-man O5, who has inside position on his defensive opponent X1. Moving the ball to the weakside man should be quick to take advantage of O5's inside position. In order to hold this inside position, the player should have a wide stance. The arms should be bent at the elbows and extended. The post-player should remain in a low position with a slightly backward lean. The only way the defensive player can secure a better position is to make contact or foul his opponent.

Diagram 22-3 shows another variation of the same alignment, only this time O1 passes to O3, who has beaten his man X4 into the lane for the pass. (If O3 was not open, then O1 could have lobbed a pass to O5 with no weakside interference.) Player O3 then passes to O5 for a possible lay-up shot.

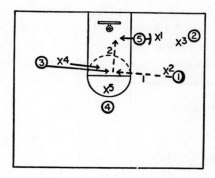

Diagram 22-3

Post-Man With Inside Position
Scoring Against a Zone

The opportunities for post-men to take and hold an inside position against defensive zone post-men are similar to the man-to-man tactics. The next three diagrams, 22-4, 22-5, and 22-6, will show plays from the top of the free throw circle against the 2-1-2 zone. Inside alignment positioning can be obtained against any zone with the ball at the top of the circle. This is from the wing position against the 1-3-1 alignment, and from the right baseline-sideline corner against the Flattened-out 2-3 alignment (Tip 2).

In Diagram 22-4, the offense is set in the Figure-eight attack (Tip 18). Ball handler O2 passes to high post-man O4. Player O4 can pass directly to O5, who has inside position on X1, or pass to the left weakside wing man O3, who can relay the ball to O5. This second pass pattern forces X4 to guard O3, eliminating weakside defensive help.

The 1-3-1 wing alignment is vulnerable to the direct pass from a wing man. (Notice in Diagram 22-5 that right wing man O2 passes directly to low post-man O5.) If accessible, pass to high post-man O4 first, who could then pass to O5. A fake pass to O3 by O4 would force X5 to move toward O3, eliminating weakside defensive help. Actually, O4 could also pass to O3, who would in turn pass to O5.

It is more difficult passing against the Flattened-out 2-3 from the backline-sideline corner. However, it is possible to lob pass inside as shown in Diagram 22-6. Player O3 has the ball in the corner, then O3 fakes a pass to O2, and then lobs the ball over X4 and X1 to O5. Player O4 keeps X5 busy by moving near the basket in a passing lane between O3 and himself. It is also possible for O3 to pass to O4, who could in turn pass to O5 under the basket.

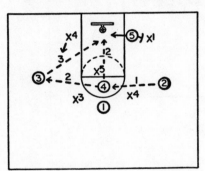

Diagram 22-4

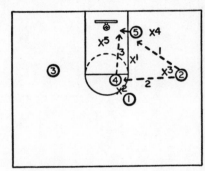

Diagram 22-5

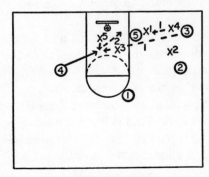

Diagram 22-6

COACHING POINTS

1. Post-players should vary their positions from inside to ball side of the defensive player to keep that player off balance.

2. The inside low-post position is excellent for rebounding shots attempted by a weakside wing or a corner shooter.

3. The outside players should always be aware of the low post-man's positioning.

4. When a high post-man establishes inside position, any player near the basket should move out to the wing positions. A pass can be made to the post-man directly from the point-player or via a weakside wing man.

5. Use fake passes in order to set up a pass to the post-man holding an inside position.

6. Placing the best shooter on the weakside wing against man-to-man forces the opponents to guard him, taking away weakside help. Against a zone, the player guarding that area is also limited in helping on the weak side.

7. Once a post-man receives the pass inside the three-second lane, he should shoot rather quickly. This should lead to possible three-point plays in addition to avoiding three-second lane violations.

8. Power lay-ups, not finesse shots, should be attempted near the basket.

TIP 23

Maneuvers to Strengthen Offensive Rebounding

OVERVIEW

Probably the least emphasis of any major phase of basketball is placed on offensive rebounding. When rebounding is mentioned, most coaches automatically think of defensive rather than offensive rebounding. Defensive rebounding is of course extremely important, but equally important is offensive rebounding. A survey of some of our game records shows that a team may shoot for a 45 to 50 percent average on first shot attempts. However, second shot attempts are successful over 70 percent of the time. (This changes the points per possession rather drastically.) Also, there are twice as many fouls leading to three-point plays on second and third shot attempts. Strong offensive rebounding can frustrate and psychologically upset a defensive team because it leads to retaining ball possession and also being able to score on shots close to the basket. Strong offensive boardwork impedes the opponent's fast break because it eliminates the defensive rebound, which is the very foundation of the fast break.

The following four points should be considered in the planning of offensive rebounding: First, make players aware of offensive rebounding positioning while running the offensive pattern. Second, use the spot rebounding positioning theory with the player shooting and the player rebounding relationship (Tip 9). Third, send three players to the boards on each shot with two back to maintain defensive balance. (One of the two players has the option to stay at the free throw line to retrieve high rebounds or to retreat back to a defensive position.) The fourth and final point is to use team and individual tactics to gain and maintain good rebounding positioning (Tip 9).

129

EXECUTION

The maneuvers to be discussed are adaptable to any man-to-man or zone type of offense. Two underlying rules make this possible. The first is "when the shot begins, the pattern stops," followed by the previously mentioned second rule, which is when the shot is attempted, "three players should move toward the boards and two should move back." Players should scramble to the most logical rebounding positions. They should hold these positions until ready to rebound the ball.

When rebounding, five basic rules prevail: (1) When a rebound and the ball are close to the basket, tip the ball toward the basket with one or both hands; (2) If an easy tip is not possible, then grab the ball and bring it down. Next, proceed to jump to shoot or fake a shot and shoot. An exception might be to pass to a teammate on the opposite side of the basket; (3) Be conscious of the three-second rule; (4) If you cannot tip the ball towards the basket or grab it, then tip it out to any teammate, even one of the players further from the basket; (5) For rebounds away from the basket, grab the ball. If this is not possible, then tip to a teammate.

With these rules, along with tactics from Tip 9 in mind, follow the maneuvers in Diagrams 23-1 through 23-4.

Offensive Rebounding
Against the Man-to-Man

Diagram 23-1 displays a method of rebounding after a wing man's shot, following a Two-player stack play. Player O4 screens for O3 from their double low stack positions on the right block (low-post) area. Meanwhile, O1, the ball handler at the top of the free throw circle, passes to right wing man O2. Player O2 passes to O3 on the right side, who in turn should shoot. Player O5 fills the weakside rebound position, O4 the center position, and O2 moves to the right side rebounding position. Shooter O3 moves toward the right side of the free throw line. (O3 does not have to follow his shot; instead he should cover the high outside area.) Player O1 stays back on defense.

The highlight of the next maneuver shown in Diagram 23-2 involves weakside exchange-screens. This screen sets up a better weakside board coverage. In the diagram, O1 drives toward the basket from the right side of the free throw circle; O1 then stops and

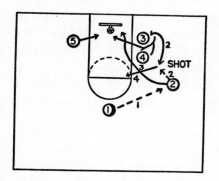

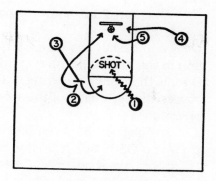

Diagram 23-1   Diagram 23-2

shoots a jump shot. Right low post-man O5 fights to occupy the center rebound position. Player O4 moves from a right corner position to the right side of the basket. Meanwhile, O3 and O2 reverse on the weak side. However, in reversing, it is better to use screens occasionally to either free a player going to the basket or free a player moving to the guard position. The rule is to up-screen when the exchange takes place above the free throw line extended and to set a down-screen if the reverse takes place below the free throw line extended. In the diagram, O3 sets an up-screen, freeing O2 to race to the basket for a pass or, in this case, a rebound position on the left side of the basket. Player O3 is back on defense and O1, the shooter, stays in the free throw area looking for a high rebound.

Offensive Rebounding Against Zones

Although zone defenses are geared for stronger defensive rebounding by stationing players near the basket, the players often forget to ward off the oncoming offensive rebounders. Zone defenses often allow the zone offense to station a post-man near the basket in excellent rebounding position.

The rebounding positioning with the ball at the top of the free throw circle is similar to rebounding against the man-for-man defense using the two underlying rules to combat the many different zone alignments possible (for example, 2-1-2, 3-2, 1-3-1). However, with the ball on a wing (forcing the defense into a 1-3-1 alignment, or with the zone in a Flattened-out 2-3 when the ball is in a baseline-sideline corner), it becomes easier to plan rebound tactics (Tip 2).

Diagram 23-3 shows rebounding after a shot from the right wing. Right wing O1 shoots. Weakside player O3 occupies the weakside basket position, O5 quickly moves from a high-post position to the middle position in front of the basket. Right corner player O4 fills the right side of the basket position. Meanwhile, shooter O1 covers the right side of the free throw line area and O2 stays back on defense.

In Diagram 23-4 the ball is in the right corner in O1's possession, and O5 is being fronted in this right low-post position. When O1 shoots, weakside man O4 attempts to obtain a rebounding position on the weak side. Player O5 fills the middle position, O2 the basket right side, and O1 goes to the right side of the free throw line, while O3 goes back on defense. (With quick movements, O2, O4, and O5 can outnumber the defensive rebounders since X1 is fronting O5.)

Finally, if the zone is in Convergence alignment (Tip 2), the offensive players should look for open lanes leading to rebound positions and use individual tactics to obtain them. The defensive players should be concentrating on stopping the shot or pass, making it possible for the offensive players to obtain better rebounding positions.

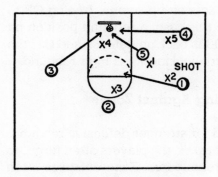

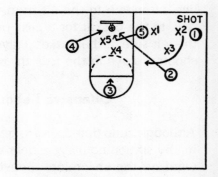

Diagram 23-3   Diagram 23-4

COACHING POINTS

1. Anticipation of the shot triggers the struggle for positioning by the potential offensive rebounders.

2. Quickness in reaching the height of a jump is more important than the height of the jumper.

3. When the ball is shot, an offensive player should **either be a rebounder or play back** for a possible rebound or be ready to go on defense.

4. Plan your offensive rebounding attacks and practice them often.

5. If a player is not able to secure a rebound position, he should keep the opponent busy blocking out so that the opponent cannot rebound the ball.

6. A player should time his jump to tap or grab the ball at the highest point possible.

7. When practicing rebounding drills, use toughness drills, speed-jumping drills, high jumping drills, and tapping drills.

8. The rebounding formula is: intense effort, consistent effort, positioning, timing, and quick jumping. If properly applied, this formula should result in successful offensive rebounding.

TIP 24

Inside-Outside-Inside Method For Executing Offensive Baseline Out-of-Bounds Plays

OVERVIEW

The offensive Baseline out-of-bounds play is a special situation that is vital to winning games. The plays usually occur close to the basket, emphasizing the importance of designing fundamentally sound, quick scoring maneuvers to take advantage of the location of the play.

The successful out-of-bounds plays should constitute several options, strategic use of players, and teamwork to lead to baskets against both the man-to-man and zone defenses.

Once again, quick scoring should be a prime offensive goal. It is easier to set up a close-in high percentage shot from an out-of-bounds play under the basket than from a regular offensive pattern. Therefore, take advantage of this situation and avoid wasting extra effort and energy. Besides, a quick scoring play gives a team a psychological advantage. The Inside-outside-inside method of attacking in this situation is a sure method of creating high percentage shots which should result in more baskets.

EXECUTION

There are many offensive formations for Offensive-baseline out-of-bounds plays. The Box, The I, The Horizontal line, The Diagonal set, and The Scattered set are some of the more common ones. The Inside-outside-inside method of offensing can integrate into many formations, with some limited adjustments. Probably the first choice would be to attempt to secure a position inside the defense. The second choice would be to take advantage of the defensive team's adjustments to stop the inside attempt by striking from the outside perimeter. The third choice would be to move the ball inside again to counteract the defensive adjustments to cut off the outside shot (most teams usually try the first two choices).

Inside-Outside-Inside Method
Against Man-to-Man Defense

The best way to execute an offensive thrust while attempting to score inside against a man-to-man defense is to use Two-man-interchanges (screen and roll-in maneuvers). This Interchange maneuver clears a player after a well-executed screen, or with the Roll-in maneuver in case the "switch" is made by the two defensive players. Diagrams 24-1 and 24-2· show the Inside-outside-inside method. (The offensive formation will be displayed as a box in all the plays.)

In Diagram 24-1, pivot player O5 has the ball ready to inbound it. A big man should inbound the ball, as he will usually end up being the inside man. Players O3 and O4 are positioned on each side of the free throw line. Players O1 and O2 stand on each side and near the top of the free throw circle. Player O5 signals to start the play. This can be done by slapping the ball or by just saying the word "Go." Player O3 jab-steps left, then sets an inside-lateral-screen (Tip 6) for player O4. Player O4 jab-steps right, then cuts left

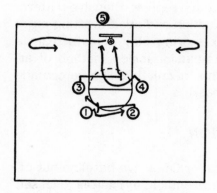

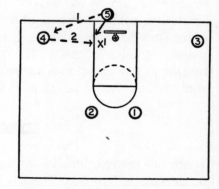

Diagram 24-1   Diagram 24-2

to the basket off O3's screen. Player O3 rolls in right to the basket. If neither player receives a pass, O4 quickly moves to the left corner and sets up for a jump shot. Player O3 does the same in the right corner. Meanwhile, O2 sets a screen for O1, who moves to the opposite side of the circle. Either O1 or O2 may break for the basket if an opening is available. Up to this point, the inside and outside maneuvers have been implemented. Passes in order would be to O4 or O3 on the screen-and-roll play. Second would be a pass to either player in the corners.

The second inside movement is shown in Diagram 24-2, which is a continuation of Diagram 24-1. Pivot-man O5 passes to O4 in the left corner; O5 then quickly takes advantage of a common temporary delayed reaction by X1 to move to the left low-post position for a return pass by O4 for a drive toward the basket, or a shot attempt by O5. (A fake pass by O5 to any other teammate makes this play easier.)

Passing to one side and moving to the opposite low-post as shown in Diagram 24-3 is another way to move the ball inside. Player O5 passes to O4 in the left corner, then O5 moves to the right low-post position. The ball is passed around the perimeter from O4 to O2 to O3. Player O3 then passes in to O5 for the offensive move or shot.

Multiple-screen-and-roll-in plays work like magic at leading to the relatively easy lay-in shot. An example of a Multiple-screen play is shown in Diagram 24-4. Players O4 initiates the play by up-screening for O2. Player O2 uses the screen to cut to the right side. Player O4 reverse-turns right to move toward the basket. Mean-

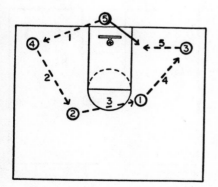

Diagram 24-3

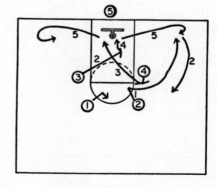

Diagram 24-4

while, O3 has set an inside-lateral-screen for O4, freeing O4 to receive a pass to shoot a lay-up. Player O3 rolls-in and is also ready to shoot. If neither player receives a pass, then O3 should move to the right corner vacated by O2, and player O4 should move to the left corner. Meanwhile, O1 should stay near the top of the circle. The team is now ready for a pass out or back inside if a shot does not take place in the sequence of movements.

Inside-Outside-Inside Method
Against Zone Defense

Most teams play a zone defense (usually a 2-3) to protect against the interchange and screening maneuvers and thus to better protect the internal area. Diagrams 24-5 and 24-6 show how to implement this method against the zone. The box formation is again set up, only this time a guard (the best shooter) takes the ball out-of-bounds. Players O5 and O4 cut to the basket (one on each side of the defensive center), looking for a pass. Player O3 cuts to the left corner at the same time, while O2 takes the point position. Player O1 passes to O3, then goes to the right side. Player O3 passes to O2, who passes to O1 (any perimeter player may shoot if open), while O4 goes to the right low-post and O5 to the left low-post. Both are ready to receive a pass inside.

Diagram 24-6 shows the inside pass from O1 to low post-man O4 as the play continues. Player O4 is in position to make a move or to shoot.

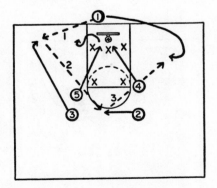

Diagram 24-5

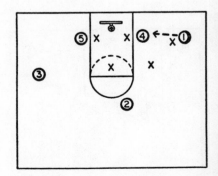

Diagram 24-6

COACHING POINTS

1. The player inbounding the ball should make a quick, sharp pass.

2. A player should break the pattern only in case there is an excellent opportunity to score a lay-up.

3. The player inbounding the ball should look for quick moves to occupy a low-post position.

4. Setting and using screens followed by the rolling-in maneuvers should be executed with precision; the players should be patient and should not rush.

5. Good floor balance is part of any out-of-bounds play.

6. Good rebounding positions should be part of the out-of-bounds play.

7. A cutter moving inside against a zone defense receiving the ball should make a strong move to shoot a lay-up and look for a three-point play.

8. Look for a high pass and **sky-shot** (a dunk or lay-in where the player catches **and** shoots while in the air) when possible.

TIP 25

Control Tempo and Score
More Lay-Ups
With the Floater Delay
Man-to-Man Offense

OVERVIEW

More emphasis than ever is being placed on game tempo at both the high school and the college levels. High school teams do not use the 24-second or 30-second clocks used in professional basketball and in the international games. Some college leagues are experimenting with 30-second and 45-second clocks during the regular season competition, but not in post season tournaments. Even when a time clock is used, this offense can be effective if combined with the Automatic twenty-second offense (Tip 17). High school and college teams do not have any restrictions against zone or a combination man-to-man and zone defenses. This offers opportunity for the use of slowdown tactics. The tempo range can vary from very slow and deliberate to a consistently fast-breaking, quick-shooting offense.

The tempo control factor of a game is usually influenced more by the offensive phase than the defensive phase. A team may possess the ball for long intervals before attempting to score, whereas it cannot dictate to the same degree the length of time prior to a shot by the opponent. Consequently, the discussion will center on the control of the tempo with various offensive strategies.

There is a difference between Tempo control basketball and Tempo tampering basketball. Tempo control is a situation when a team plays its own style and tempo of basketball directly related to player abilities and potential of the opponent. Tempo tampering is slowing down the offensive pace when the opponents have inferior personnel.

141

General strategies in basketball should center on the abilities of players of each team in relation to the opponent. Teams composed of highly skilled players should utilize all phases of offense to score. The transition break and quick-scoring patterns and free lance plays should be used by the offensive team. On defense, the outstanding team should use pressure and run tactics. However, if a team has players of inferior abilities, then the slowdown Tempo control methods should be installed in order to attempt to limit the scoring potential of a superior opponent. (However, slowdown offensive patterns may be used by either team late in the first half when playing for the last shot. This might also be true late in the game when trying to protect a slim lead.) Beware of Tempo tampering, because the rhythm change from fast to slow, deliberate basketball limits the scoring potential of the players and gives the weaker opponent an opportunity to keep the score close and to build momentum, which is important in controlling any basketball game.

This cautious approach by coaches is increasing at an alarming rate. Coaches direct teams to change tempo after taking a lead, particularly in the second half, with considerable playing time left. Once a team has used the slowdown tactics, it is difficult for the team to bring the tempo back to its original level of speed.

All teams should be well-prepared to play any phase or tempo of the offensive game. The versatile team utilizes what is demanded in accordance with the game situation. Slowdown tactics should be a game plan rule for weaker teams and should be practiced often. Teams should be proficient in using a sound pattern with patience leading to either ball control or to an easy basket. Also, to win consistently a team should be able to maintain and eventually increase a lead during the final two minutes of a game. The key to tempo control is constant practice in the offensive ball control phase of basketball.

EXECUTION

Use the Floater offense against the more powerful teams using man-to-man pressure methods (with either the opponents slightly ahead or behind by a small margin). It is ideal to use when ahead late in the game. It offers more benefits than the popular Four-corners attack because the floater attack absorbs the Four-corner tactics of penetrating and shooting, or passing off, **plus it gives players more room to maneuver near the basket** with cuts and back-door plays. A detailed description of the Floater will follow because it is considered a newly designed attack.

Diagram 25-1 shows the Floater set-up. Player O1 is the point-man, usually the ball handling guard, who can penetrate, drive and pass off, or shoot. This player must be able to dribble to keep possession of the ball. Players O2 and O3 are the other guard and small forward (the next two most agile players). Players O4 and O5 are the two biggest players, usually a forward and a center. The set-up is like a 1-4 stack offense, except that the stacks are set up near the top of the free throw circle extended, approximately six feet from the sidelines. The spread concept, away from the basket, is relatively new. This open position gives more room for players to move under the basket with or without the ball. The open floater stack concept offers the players an opportunity to deceive the opponents or set up screens. Players O2 and O3 can use stack players O4 and O5 to maneuver free for a drive toward the basket or for a release pass away from the basket. The main objective is to spread the defense, which will establish opportunities for lay-up shots while moving the larger defensive players away from the basket area. This offense allows for floor balance and ball control measures if scoring opportunities are not present, which is another advantage.

Some of the key movements are depicted in the following diagrams. Diagram 25-2 shows O1 with ball driving to the basket. If O1 can drive by his opponent, the lay-up is available; if not, player O3 sets a screen for O5, who cuts to the basket for a possible pass. Player O3 could also make a straight cut toward the basket. Meanwhile, player O4 screens for player O2 in order that O2 would be available for a pressure release pass if needed. It is also possible for O1 to pass to any player open on either side, then break for the basket to receive a return pass for a lay-up.

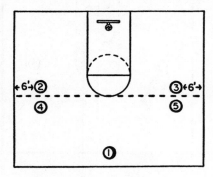

Diagram 25-1

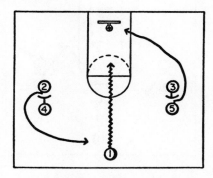

Diagram 25-2

The Back-door play is depicted in Diagram 25-3. Player O3 sets an up-screen for O5 to cut to the basket. Player O5 starts toward the basket, then cuts to the free throw line for a pass from O1. Meanwhile, O3 cuts to the basket for a pass from O5 for a lay-up. Players O2 and O4 break out of the stack after a screen play, but stay wide on the court.

In Diagram 25-4, the Triangle-cut is displayed. Player O1 penetrates to the free throw line, while O2 up-screens for O4 and O3 up-screens for O5. Players O4 and O5 drive toward the basket to set up a fast break triangle (as O2 and O3 drop back).

In Diagram 25-5, the Give-and-go is displayed. Player O1 passes to O4 after O4 Down-screens-and-rolls. Player O1 then moves towards O4. Then O1 makes a quick cut toward the basket for a return pass from O4. On the opposite side, O5 down-screens for O3 and then moves to the release area, after which O5 moves towards the basket.

In the final diagram, 25-6, the Screen-and-go, O2 moves out, helped by a down-screen from O4, to receive a pass from O1. Player O1 then cuts down the middle and after O5 screens for O3 to pop up, O1 then also screens for O3. Player O3 breaks to the basket for a pass and shot. Player O5 could also receive the screen from O1 for a cut, depending upon which defensive player appears most vulnerable. The players can find more opportunities for scoring if they stay wide, time their cuts, and keep setting the proper screens. Setting **legal** screens is important. Careless screens are of little value because the defensive players have to watch the ball and the other players spread over half the court, thereby making it difficult for the defensive players to follow the quick movements made by the offensive players, even without the screens.

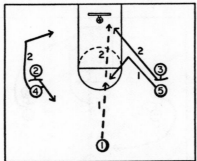
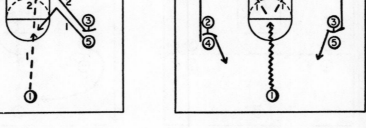

Diagram 25-3   **Diagram 25-4**

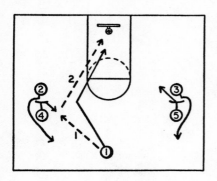

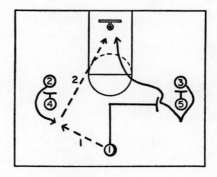

Diagram 25-5   **Diagram 25-6**

COACHING POINTS

1. A good team should attempt to change tempos without affecting scoring momentum.

2. Scoring momentum is best maintained by **making free throw attempts.**

3. Patience will give the defensive players time to make mistakes leading to relatively easy baskets by the offense.

4. Any of the five players can be potential scorers with the Floater offense.

5. Utilize a good ball handling tall player at the top, especially against a weak defensive player.

6. Try to pass the ball to the weakest defender's opponent, who in turn should drive toward the basket.

7. If a player drives to the basket and does not have an opportunity to shoot a lay-up, that player should continue to dribble, moving out of the shooting area and then passing it to a release man.

.8 The player handling the ball should know where the other nine players are located on the court.

TIP 26

Regaining Lost Momentum

OVERVIEW

Momentum in a basketball game generally refers to a team pushing ahead or having impetus to score points and also play outstanding defense.

Each game is an entity in itself. Game patterns tend to vary to some degree. A superior team playing an inferior one will win a greater share of the time. It is a different situation when two teams with approximately equal ability are trying to gain and maintain scoring momentum necessary to win a game. Perhaps one team will gain a comfortable lead, then later in the game, the opponent will attempt to overcome this lead. Perhaps both teams have scoring momentum at various times throughout the contest. Or perhaps neither team has scoring momentum during the greater part of the game, then suddenly one team scores several consecutive points to win in the last few minutes. The object of the game is to be consistent on both defense and offense and for your team to maintain a scoring pace that will insure victory.

There is usually a specific cause for the gain or the loss of momentum. Once you understand this concept, you are ready to begin your analysis of why the opponent has gained momentum and why you have lost it. This tip will focus on regaining lost momentum (overcoming a dry spell in scoring), with some reference made to stopping the opponent's impetus.

EXECUTION

When a team is performing rhythmically and scoring consistently, then suddenly stops, it is important to quickly analyze the situation

147

and make the necessary correct adjustments before the team either loses a lead or permits an opponent to turn a close game into a rout.

Assuming that a team has sufficient ability to regain momentum, then it would be a good policy to make the necessary positive adjustments. First listed will be the positive momentum adjustments. Then a **Problem Chart** will be developed depicting the cause of the momentum loss, followed by positive steps to re-establish momentum. You can use the chart to select any or all adjustments in any order.

Positive Adjustments

A. Change pressure or use a drop-back defense.

B. Use a pressing defense.

C. Change defensive man-to-man assignments.

D. Make adjustments in a defense to stop a hot shooter.

E. Exercise more patience on offense.

F. Look for the inside type of shots or lay-ups.

G. Look for short jump shots.

H. Attempt to fast break more often.

I. Use a better shot selection.

J. Use more passing and player movement before the shot attempt.

K. Give the ball to a particular player.

L. Make key substitutions.

M. Call a time out to discuss problems.

N. Use a delayed type of offense.

O. Play the best ball handlers.

P. Substitute a taller player(s).

Q. Use the most poised players.

R. Try a trick type of play.

S. Look for charge-taking opportunities.

The problem chart lists the situations causing the loss of momentum. The letter of the positive action statement listed above will follow the problem situation. Any or several of the positive actions may be appropriate for use in attempting to eliminate the problem or problems.

Problem Chart

1. For a team that is overanxious, use E, F, G, I, J, K, L, M, and Q.
2. Opponents on a hot shooting streak, use A, B, C, D, E, J, M, and S.
3. Opponents beating the pressure defense, use A.
4. When a team is sluggish, use B, H, J, L, M.
5. When a team is making poor shooting selection, use E, F, G, I, J, K, L, M, N.
6. When shooting a low percentage, use B, E, F, H, J, K, R, S.
7. In a tough game caused by loose officiating, use B, E, F, G, H, I, L, N, Q.
8. When a team has been guilty of excessive turnovers, use E, F, G, H, I, J, L, M, O, Q.
9. If poor ball handling is displayed, use L, M, O, Q, S.
10. When a team is in foul trouble, use A, C, D, E, F, G, I, J, L, M, N.
11. When players are fatigued, use A, C, E, F, G, I, K, L, M, N, O, P, S.
12. When injury to a key player occurs, use A, C, E, F, G, I, J, L, M, N.
13. When inside shooters are getting roughed, use E, G, H, I, J, M, N, R.
14. When poor offensive rebounding occurs, use A, B, C, L, P, S.
15. When not finishing the fast break, use G, I, L, M, O, Q.
16. When the offensive rhythm is erratic, use E, F, G, H, I, J, K, L, M.
17. When the opponents change defense, use E, F, G, H, I, J, K, L, M.
18. If an opponent switches to a pressure defense, use H, S, M, O, Q.
19. When a team is not executing offensive patterns properly, use H, J, L, M, O.
20. When substitutes are having difficulty finding rhythm, use E, F, G, I, K, L, M.
21. If offensive rebounding is inadequate, use E, F, G, H, I, J, L, P.

COACHING POINTS

1. Attempt to make adjustments with the game in progress rather than using extra time-outs.

2. Use a pressure defense to off-set the opponent's patterned offensive momentum; this will give your team more scoring opportunities.

3. Avoid hasty changes if the team happens to have a cold shooting spell despite taking good shots.

4. Know the ability of the players and use them wisely.

5. Try to maneuver to an inside position to draw shooting fouls or attempt to make three-point plays prior to the bonus fouls.

6. Check the statistic chart at halftime or during the game to find any oversight in analyzing the game problems.

7. A touch of humor at the right time can be very helpful.

8. Don't panic if your team cannot score for a few minutes. Be confident and encourage the players to stay calm.

TIP 27

Special Plays
For Last Second Scoring

OVERVIEW

Many games during a season are decided in the last few seconds. One should expect close games and prepare the team to meet the challenge of these down-to-the-wire contests, if there is any aspiration of winning a championship or having a winning season. (See the Two-minute game, Tip 32.) Only one of our many championship teams went undefeated and dominated the opponents by playing only one close game during the entire season. The remainder of our championship squads played in many close games.

There are numerous special situations which take place during a game. It would be impossible to list all of them. The purpose of this tip is to provide a team with the offensive punch needed in the most commonplace situations arising in the closing seconds of a game.

There are also many defensive situations that occur in the waning moments which require special plays when the team is behind and the opponents have the ball. The team's defense in essence becomes the offense. This is part of the defense phase and will be discussed in Tip 30.

The plays discussed here are those designed for the situations where there are five seconds or less to play and the team can tie or win the game on the last shot. The plays originate from out-of-bounds in the backcourt, out-of-bounds at midcourt, and when the ball is in play in the frontcourt. The plays to be discussed are in addition to the ones utilized on a regular basis. This will be explained further as each play is described.

EXECUTION

Some general comments are necessary prior to the explanations of the last second plays. Let us assume we have a game with one minute remaining and a team is two or less points behind. Should the team attempt to score immediately or try for the last shot?

The law of averages favors the team trying to score as soon as possible, rather than delay the shot. Even when considering the various aspects, such as type of game, opponents' strength, the refereeing, whether it is at home or on the road game, etc., I would rather force the action. If the score is tied, then run the clock down to ten seconds, call a time-out, set up a play, then take the shot with two seconds left. This minimizes the possibility of the opponent getting the ball for a last shot.

The first two plays originate from out-of-bounds at the offensive backcourt baseline. The Pushover is the first play. It may be tried with two time-outs available. This is especially desirable with two or fewer seconds left in the game. The play is shown in Diagram 27-1. O1 has the ball after a basket has been scored. O2 and O3 line up near each other facing O1. Players O4 and O5 are slightly beyond midcourt on the left side. The strategy of this play is to try leading X2 into a charging foul by bumping into O3 (the best free throw shooter). Following the action in the diagram, O1 takes one step left, runs right four steps along the baseline, as O3 moves to set an inside-lateral-screen near the baseline. Player X2 guards O1, trying to prevent a pass inbounds, and charges into O3 for the foul. (If this does not work, O1 must call time-out immediately to avoid a four-second count violation. Meanwhile, O5 and O4 reverse to create nuisance movement.

Diagram 27-2 shows an offense to inbound the ball from the defensive baseline for a possible quick score following a time-out, with three to five seconds left to play in the half or game. The Ten-second last shot offense (Tip 28) works well if there are not any time-outs left. A tall player O3 should be ready to inbound the ball, with O4, O5, and O2 set up at the free throw line facing O3. Player O1, the best ball handler, is near the top of the circle. On the predetermined signal, O1 moves toward O3 to receive the ball. Suddenly O1 cuts off a down-screen set by O4 and races at maximum speed toward the basket to receive a pass from O3 for a shot. If O1 is not clear, then the ball should be passed to O2 (the second best ball handler) who should dribble at maximum speed

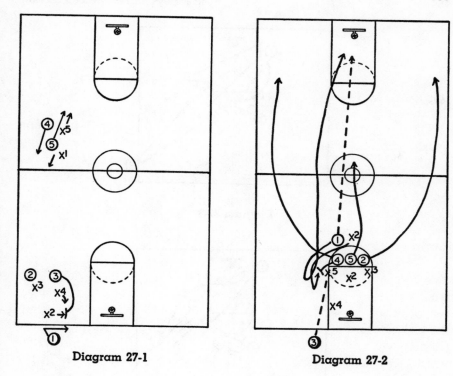

Diagram 27-1   Diagram 27-2

toward the basket to take a shot. Notice the routes of the other players. They should also move up-court quickly when the ball is passed. It is logical to move the ball close to the basket before trying the final shot. If there is sufficient time, then this should be planned, especially if the defensive team does not pressure fullcourt.

The next two diagrams show the A and B special series plays, which are out-of-bounds plays executed at midcourt.

The Special series A play, with one to three seconds left (note Diagram 27-3) has O2 with the ball at right side midcourt. Player O5 is to the right of the free throw line extended. Player O1 (the best shooter) is at the left block while O3 is on the left side near the top of the free throw circle, and O4 is on the right side. Players O3, O4 and O5 set a triple-screen for O1, who jab-steps, then moves to the free throw area for a pass from O2 for the shot. Players O3, O4, and O5 move towards the basket for a pass from O2 if necessary, and to rebound while O2 moves to a jump shooting position after passing the ball.

The Special series B play takes place with one second left on the clock. The players are in the same formation as in the previous

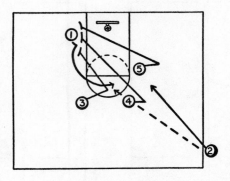

Diagram 27-3

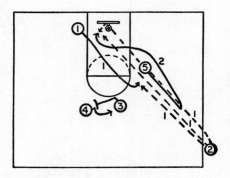

Diagram 27-4

play. Player O5 (big player, or exceptional jumper) moves towards O2, turns, and races to exchange positions with O1, who moves towards O2. If O1 is open, he receives the pass for the shot; if O5 is clear, he receives a lob pass for a sky-shot.

Another variation to this play is for the ball to be passed off the backboard with O5 jumping to either tip it into the basket or retrieving it, then quickly shooting a lay-up (note Diagram 27-4).

The next two plays originate with two to five seconds remaining on the clock after the ball has been inbounded against a man-to-man defense. (The Automatic twenty-second man offense—Tip 17—works well here also.)

The players are in a two back and three up front offensive formation (see Diagram 27-5). Right guard O1 passes to right wing man O4. Meanwhile, left wing man O3 (best shooter and driver) breaks off an outside-lateral-screen set by high post-man O5. Player

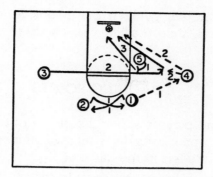

Diagram 27-5

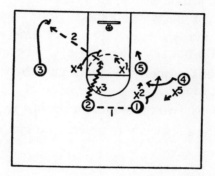

Diagram 27-6

O3 may receive a pass for the shot behind the screen, or he can continue down the right side of the lane to receive a pass for a lay-up. Meanwhile, O5 rolls to the basket if O3 receives a pass near the free throw area. Player O5 should stay at the high-post for a pass if O3 continues cutting to the basket. Players O1 and O2 reverse to keep the defense from sagging. (O4 can also shoot if he cannot pass to another player.)

The second play (the same formation as the previous one) is the Weakside corner shot play, Diagram 27-6. Player O1 has the ball and passes to O2, the best driver, ball handler, and a good shooter. Players O1 and O4 crisscross, keeping their opponents from sagging. Player O1 then drives toward the basket as O3 (best shooter) moves to the left corner area. If O2 cannot drive to the basket, he or she passes to O3 for the shot. Player O3 should be open momentarily when defender X4 attempts to help X3 guard against O2's drive.

Another important point: If the defensive team is in a drop-back zone defense, then the Figure-eight zone offense should be used (Tip 18).

COACHING POINTS

1. Coach and players should be aware of the score, time remaining, opponent's defense, own offense, and the number of time-outs left in the game.

2. Try to use players' strengths in crucial situations.

3. Have several alternate moves off each play.

4. Plan a shot to score; include rebounding positioning rather than only a desperation shot.

5. Five second is a longer period of time than most players realize. Do not rush the play and especially not the shot.

6. Set screens properly to avoid any chance of an offensive charging foul.

7. Save at least two time-outs for the last two minutes of play.

8. Make sure a shot is attempted on a last second play.

TIP 28

The Ten-Second Last Shot Offense After Opponent's Free Throws

OVERVIEW

A formal offense after gaining ball possession following missed or made free throw attempts in the closing seconds of a game is an invaluable weapon when a basket is needed to tie or to win the game. We have had considerable success using the Ten-second offense in these critical situations. This offense is mandatory, as there are usually free throw situations in the last few seconds of a close game. This formal attack works best when play is continuous. If planned, it is not necessary to use a precious timeout. All players are continually being reminded of their assignments, thereby eliminating any confusion. The attack is used when there are ten seconds or less left in the game to set up a last shot against any type of defense. Normally, however, the opponent will be in a pressure man-for-man defense in this situation.

The ten-second attack offers the following five important ingredients for a successful attack. First, a team can position players to take advantage of the good ball handlers and the best shooter(s). Second, the ball can be moved up-court rapidly. Third, there are several alternatives in moving the ball up-court. Fourth, there are alternate opportunities for the last shot. And fifth, there is good rebounding positioning involved in the attack.

EXECUTION

The object of this offense is to take a good high percentage last shot. Time is of the essence at this point. The more time available, the better the shot selection should be. Rebounding is also available in each situation should there be enough time remaining to tap in an errant shot attempt.

Although the basic offensive formation is quite similar, the player movements can change once the attack is initiated. Diagram 28-1 shows the basic formation and movement leading to the sideline pass maneuver. Player O4 is the left side first position rebounder. Player O5, the better all-around player of the two, assumes that position on the right side. (They should be the two best rebounders on the team.) Player O1, the best ball handling guard, is at the third rebound position on the left side. Player O3 should be the best all-around player of the big men. He should be positioned three feet from the top of the offensive free throw circle. Player O2, the best outside shooter, is positioned about twenty feet from O3 and near the center-court circle. The action in the diagram shows player O4 possessing the ball after a missed free throw attempt. Player O4 passes it to O1 flaring out to an outlet spot on the leftside, then doubling back for the pass. Player O5 moves up-court at maximum speed. Meanwhile, O3 and O2 reverse, with O3 going to

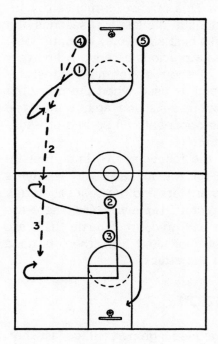

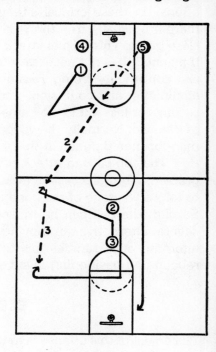

Diagram 28-1   Diagram 28-2

the left sideline area just inside the offensive frontcourt, and O2 moves to inside the free throw line, turns left, and races to the left-wing position. (These are the basic moves in each play.) Player O1 passes to O3, who passes it to O2 for a shot. Player O5 should be in the weakside rebounding position.

Diagram 28-2 is the same sideline play, except O5 is the rebounder and passes out to O1, who moves near the top of the free throw circle for the outlet pass. The remainder of the action is identical to the previous one.

The Dribble-drive play is shown in Diagram 28-3, with the following action taking place. Player O4 rebounds the missed free throw and passes it to outlet man O1. Player O1 dribble-drives at maximum speed to the offensive free throw line. (He can drive all the way to the basket when possible.) Player O1 can shoot or pass the ball to either O2 on the left side for a jump shot or to O5 on the right side for the lay-up.

Another version of the Dribble-drive is shown in Diagram 28-4. This time, player O3 near midcourt receives the pass from outlet-man O1, and O3 dribble-drives the ball to the free throw line.

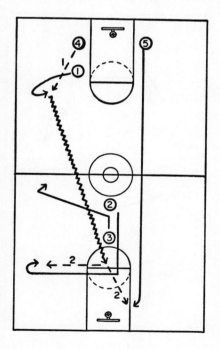

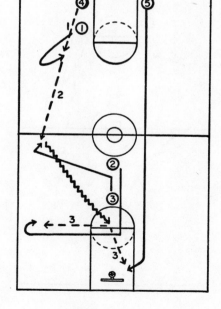

Diagram 28-3   Diagram 28-4

The same shooting alternatives are available.

The next two diagrams, 28-5 and 28-6, show the attack forming after a successful free throw attempt. This is the Opposite-side play. This time O4 takes the ball to an out-of-bounds position after the made free throw, and inbounds it to big man O5 (who moved close to midcourt, then cut back for a pass). Player O5 passes deep to shooter O2 on the right wing for the shot. Player O2 headed to the left side, then raced to the right wing, ball-side position. Meanwhile, O3 drives to the free throw area for a possible pass. If O2 shoots, then O3 should move into the weakside rebounding position. (See Digram 28-5.)

A third version of the Dribble-drive is shown in Diagram 28-6. Again, O4 inbounds the made free throw to O5 on the right near midcourt. This time O5 passes to O1, breaking to the middle from his left outlet position. O1 dribble-drives the ball near the free throw line. Meanwhile, O2 has faked going to the left side and hurries to the right-wing position. O3 drives toward the left side of the basket for a pass, lay-up shot, or a rebound.

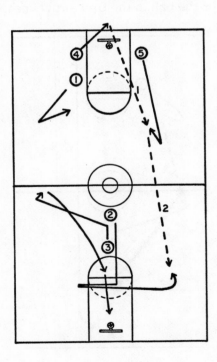

Diagram 28-5   **Diagram 28-6**

COACHING POINTS

1. Whenever player O4 rebounds or has possession of the ball, he makes the outlet pass to either O1 or O5. (Occasionally O4 may be able to throw a long pass to O3.)

2. Any player with the ball can pass it directly to O2 for a quick shot, if O2 is open.

3. Any player near the basket should look to set up a fast break triangle or to rebound a missed shot.

4. The Ten-second offense should be implemented in every practice session as a warm-up drill and also during scrimmage period.

5. Player O5 should be open quite often in this attack.

6. Use jab-step fakes and a change of direction maneuvers to secure freedom for a pass reception.

7. Always have players practice counting seconds to themselves so they can estimate the time left. This helps a player make an accurate last split-second decision to shoot. Even in practice, the shot should always be taken before the time expires.

8. Basketball players should develop a shooting rhythm that can be used in game competition. A shot made more quickly than this is usually missed.

TIP 29

Defensing the Four-Corners

OVERVIEW

Originally, the Four-corners offense was designed to use up time late in the game by a team protecting a lead. It later became a weapon used by an inferior team as a stall or semi-stall offense to prevent an opponent from having possession of the ball as often. In addition to these two purposes it is currently employed by a superior team when ahead during various times in a game to use up time while taking advantage of the weaker opponent, and to increase the lead. This dynamic attack is used by many teams for all three purposes. The advantage of this offense, made famous by Dean Smith, head coach at the University of North Carolina, and his teams, is the simplicity in learning the offense. In fact, every team should be taught the Four-corners offense. It can be used as a delay game offense as well as a ball handling drill in practice. By using this attack a team will also learn how to defense against it when employed by an opponent. This tip deals with defensing the Four-corners attack.

EXECUTION

The Four-corners against man-to-man defense has a player in each corner, with the best ball handler at midcourt handling the ball. There are two purposes. One is to attempt to score by the ball handler driving to the basket or by driving to the free throw line and then passing to a cornerman moving toward the basket. The second purpose is to maintain control of the ball by passing it back to a player near midcourt if the defensive players sag to the three-second lane attempting to stop the drive or drop-off pass. The Four corners is devastating against the zones. There are players in each corner plus a high-post player (each holding his position). The purposes are the same. However, the execution is different when the ball is being passed around so fast that it is virtually impossible to double-team the ball handler. Scoring lay-ups when a corner-man cuts to the basket, or holding the ball are relatively easy tasks. Consequently, it is virtually impossible to use a trapping zone to defense the Four-corners.

However, there are ways to break up this attack with a man-to-man defense. The essentials are:

1. Protect against the scoring by sagging.

2. Take advantage of the weakest ball handler by attempting to force him to handle the ball more.

3. Force the ball to a sideline, and make the ball handler stop dribbling. Then guard the other players closely creating a jump ball situation or by intercepting a pass.

4. Force the ball to a deep corner-man and try for an interception or create a jump ball situation.

5. Look for double-teaming situations.

These essentials will be shown and discussed in Diagrams 29-1 through 29-5.

The same basic set-up is used for each diagram. Player O1 is the best ball handler. Players O2 and O3, the second and third best ball handlers, should be located in the back corners. Players O4 and O5 are the two big players located in the deep front corners. Diagram 29-1 shows a drive by the ball handler O1, and the basic defense to stop this move. Note that X2 should stop O1 and stay with O1, looking for a five-second count leading to a jump ball. The other players should sag toward the basket area. Protect first against an easy lay-up by O1, and second against a pass to O4 or O5 for a lay-up. Also, the sagging players look to intercept an outlet pass. (This is done by jamming the passing paths.) In the diagram, O1 is stopped by X2, forcing O1 to pass back to O3.

In Diagram 29-2, O3, the third best ball handler, has the ball and is forced to the right sideline by X4. If X4 can force O3 to pick up his dribble, the defense has some advantage. If not, the defense still has an advantage with the sagging players in position to combat or intercept a pass.

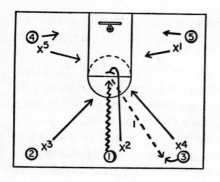

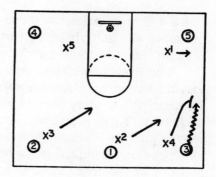

Diagram 29-1   Diagram 29-2

Diagram 29-3 shows the Corner-squeeze play. Player O1 has the ball at the middle of the court. His defender, X2, forces him to dribble right. Meanwhile, X1 loosens up to encourage a pass to deep cornerman O5 (the weakest ball handler). Player X1 puts the squeeze on O5 (after O5 receives the ball) by guarding O5 closely. Meanwhile, the other defenders do not sag toward the ball. Instead each guards his man closely to prevent or intercept a pass from O5.

The Sideline-double team can also be used effectively (Diagram 29-4). Player O1 is forced to dribble toward the right sideline. (This is the double-team key.) Player O3 clears towards the basket. Player O3's defender, X4, begins to follow O3, then turns and rushes to set a sideline-trap with X2 (O1's man). Meanwhile, X3, X5, and X1 move into the Sideline-trap alignment (Tip 4) with X3 the floater, X1 the man-in-lane, and X5 the safety-man. Should O3 pass out of the trap successfully, then the defensive players must retreat

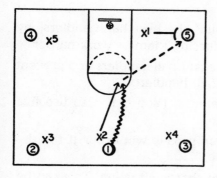

Diagram 29-3

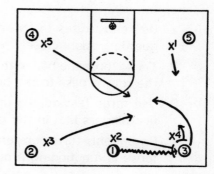

Diagram 29-4

to a 2-1-2 zone inside the three-second area temporarily, to stop an offensive thrust. When each player picks up his man again, they resume the man-to-man defense.

The Baseline-sideline trap is shown in Diagram 29-5. This trap can be set as an alternate to the Corner-squeeze play shown in Diagram 29-3. Only this time, the Baseline-sideline corner trap alignment (Tip 4) is involved with X1 and X4 trapping O5. Player X3 moves into the floater position and X2 and X5 fill the two side-by-side positions along the three-second lane. Again, if O5 releases the ball out of the trap, the defensive team retreats to a 2-1-2 zone temporarily to protect the basket area, before returning to a man-to-man defense.

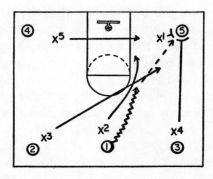

Diagram 29-5

COACHING POINTS

1. Use substitutes to "wear out" the best ball handlers, by guarding them closely and forcing them to work harder.

2. Try to force the ball to the weaker ball handlers and prevent the return pass to the best ball handler(s).

3. Use three fast guards on defense. (You may also use five fast players late in the game.)

4. Be patient; turnovers and jump balls will occur if the defense is functioning properly.

5. Always look for an **Offensive charge situation.** This can be demoralizing to a ball handler as well as teammates.

6. Use **Sagging** off-the-ball techniques when a good ball handler has the ball, and **Staying tight** on-the-ball techniques when it is handled by a weak ball handler.

7. Be ready to fast break at all times following a steal, recovery, or interception.

8. Look to cut passing lanes on each pass attempt.

TIP 30

Late Game Defensive Tactics

OVERVIEW

In a close game there is a tendency to overemphasize the offensive phase of basketball. One should be aware that in the last few minutes of play that the defense is equally if not more important than the offense. Making the right selection of defense is of prime importance. Defensive strategy can become quite involved; in fact it can be more complicated than planning the offense. The time left, the score, the good shooters, the inside game, gaining ball possession, stopping special plays, protection against inbound passes from various floor positions, preventing fast breaks, and rebounding missed shots are some of the important points to be considered. The theme of this tip involves defensive tactics to be utilized during the last two minutes of the game when a team is either winning or losing.

EXECUTION

The first part of this discussion involves defensing the last two minutes when a team is three points ahead, and the opponent has the ball. (If the advantage is four points or more, the team leading should stay with the same defense and try to build the lead with a delayed-lay-up offense.)

The standard attitude should be to maintain a rugged defense, using sound defensive principles, while omitting gambling tactics. The key strategic points whether you are using a man-to-man or a zone are:

1. Do not commit any unnecessary fouls.
2. Attempt to keep the ball away from the star player.

169

3. Do not permit the opponent to do what he wants to do.

4. Avoid three-point plays.

5. Limit the opponent to one shot by rebounding the missed attempt.

6. Look for the fast break after rebounding the missed shot.

The second part of the discussion centers on defensing the last ten seconds from various parts of the court, when one basket can tie or win the game.

If the ball is being inbounded from the defensive baseline, the key points are:

1. Man-to-man pressure on the inbound pass, without trapping.

2. Playing Ball-You-Man defense on the ball, and Ball-You-Basket off the ball (Tip 2).

3. A player in foul trouble should play hard defensively. There is not any reason to be cautious at this time.

When the ball is being inbounded at midcourt, the team should use the following defensive tactics.

1. Play the defense which appears to be most effective in a drop-back position, but keep pressure on the player with the ball. Protect the three-second area and pick up individual players immediately after the pass-in, if playing man-to-man.

2. If in a 2-1-2 zone, the front player(s) can guard the inbound pass while the back players protect the basket area.

3. Rebound a missed shot and attempt to fast break.

4. Force players to attempt outside shots, if possible somewhat beyond their shooting range.

5. Take advantage of players' weaknesses in ball handling, shooting, and individual fundamental skills.

When the ball is being inbounded under the basket along the baseline, the tactics to use are:

1. Use a 2-1-2 zone to protect the inside on the inbound pass.

2. Use the one-on-the-ball zone once the ball is inbounded.

3. Fast-break the missed shot after rebounding, except when less than five seconds remain; then retain the ball and make a sure pass away from the basket area.

The third part is playing the last two minutes when behind by three points.

The opponent will more than likely use a delayed offense. The defensive team **should force the action** by pressuring hard. Pick out the weakest free throw shooting player(s) and go after the ball attempting to steal it, without intentionally fouling. If a foul is committed, do not permit too much time to elapse. The game is played differently from that point on, depending upon whether the free throws are made or missed. Other tactics to be used:

1. Use the man-to-man defense.
2. Try doubling up on players handling the ball prior to the time that the ball crosses midcourt.
3. Use tactics suggested in Tip 29 if the opponent utilizes the Four-corners delayed game attack.
4. Be fast-break conscious while defensing.

The fourth part is defensing a team that is one or two points ahead with five seconds or less remaining, trying to inbound the ball from various court locations.

With the ball in the offensive team's backcourt, use the following tactics:

1. Play tight man-to-man on a player inbounding the ball. If possible force a corner pass.
2. Play tight man-to-man on strongside players, and sag off on the weakside players. (Play the passing lanes.)
3. Look for an opportunity to take an offensive charge.
4. Try hard to secure the ball; foul the player who receives a successful pass immediately.
5. Call time out immediately after securing the ball unless a quick basket is available.

Tactics to use if the ball is being inbounded at midcourt:

1. Play tight man-to-man defense on player inbounding the ball.

2. Play tight man-to-man on strongside players, sag off weak-side players, but play the passing lanes.

3. Stay on ball-you-man to stop any quick cut to the basket.

4. Look for an opportunity to take an offensive charge.

5. Try hard to secure the ball from the player receiving the inbounds pass. Either steal it or foul him immediately.

6. Be conscious of fast-breaking on an intercepted pass, or steal and score as quickly as possible.

7. Call time-out (if available) in order that a fast break cannot be initiated by the opponents, after you score.

The final situation is defensing the baseline under-the-basket during an inbounding play. The tactics to use are:

1. Play tight man-to-man defense on the inbounds passer.

2. Play tight man-to-man defense on other players.

3. Look for the opportunity to take an offensive charge foul on the inbound attempt.

4. Gamble for an interception.

5. Try for a steal if the ball is inbounded successfully; foul immediately in the event the steal attempt is unsuccessful.

COACHING POINTS

1. Use tenacious defense to eliminate easy lay-up shots.

2. Look for easy fast break baskets if ahead, after rebounding missed shots.

3. Use the five fastest players in the last thirty seconds if behind.

4. If the opponent scores to tie or go ahead, call time-out immediately (if available) with hopes of trying one offensive play and to attempt a good shot.

5. Try to avoid three-point plays by the opponent.

6. If ahead by three or more points with five seconds or less to play and the opponent drives for the basket, give token resistance. Permit him to shoot the lay-up unmolested to avoid a three-point play.

7. Assign a big fast player to guard an outside shooter on a last second shot. Block the shot or attempt to change the shot angle, or cause a hurried shot.

8. Attempt to force the opponent to do something that he is not equipped to accomplish.

TIP 31

Practice Short Cuts for Maximum Preparation in Minimum Time Using Two Multiple Drills

OVERVIEW

The best way to develop players and teach them the diversified intricate system of play necessary in basketball is to use the multiple weave Fundamental drill, and the Multiple control scrimmage drill. By using these two multiple drills, players practice basic fundamentals and practice the complete team system in minimum time.

The two drills should be used at least twice per week, even when the team plays twice each week, and normally two days prior to a game. These drills, along with the warmup, rebounding, shooting, late game situations, and conditioning agility drills, are quite strenuous and should not be used in the pre-game day practice. The pre-game practice day will be discussed in Tip 33.

Of course, practices vary in time and skills taught relative to early, middle, and late season. The two multiple drills to be discussed can be used throughout the season.

EXECUTION

Before going into a detailed explanation of the two multiple drills, one should reflect on some thoughts in relation to practices. The players should observe the following rules. First, when entering the gym prior to official practice, each player should do some stretching exercises to warm up, then shoot free throws while waiting for the start of the official practice. Second, players should commit themselves to a hard, strenuous, physical and mental workout. Third, the players must realize each practice is a learning experience that takes complete concentration on their part. Fourth, a team effort is necessary for a successful practice session. Fifth, players should work hard and hustle continually in practice as they should in game competition. In fact, in comparison, the game should be relatively easy compared to practice. Sixth, practice sessions should be fun and enjoyable for the players, even with the expenditure of tremendous effort and energy.

The practice time necessary for the complete workout including the two multiple drills is two hours. This is sufficient time to cover all of the essentials thoroughly. One can practice other phases of the game with other drills occasionally, in place of one or both multiple drills. The time can be cut back to an hour and forty-five minutes as the season progresses, by cutting five minutes off the multiple weave drill and ten minutes off the multiple control scrimmage.

The breakdown of time by drills follows:

Stretching exercise	5 minutes
Four ball lay-ups	5 minutes
Multiple weave drill	20 minutes
Two man jump shooting	10 minutes
Multiple control scrimmage drill	50 minutes
Free throw shooting and "The Ten second offense"	10 minutes
Two minute game	10 minutes
Abilities (touch line)	3 minutes
Five consecutive free throws	7 minutes

The two multiple drills will be discussed in detail. The other drills are standard for most teams and need not be explained.

The Fundamental Multiple Weave Drill

This drill includes most of the basic offense and defense fundamentals used in any team system of play. The first part of the drill is a three-, four-, or six-man pass and cut weave. The second part of the drill includes most of the basic individual fundamentals or fundamental plays. For example, the drill begins with a weave and ends up with a shot, a 1-on-1 play, a 2-on-1 play, etc. There are twelve different individual fundamentals or fundamental plays at the end of the weave.

Diagram 31-1 shows the three-man weave which finishes with six basic shots. The weave is the standard pass and go behind. It starts with O1 passing to O2 on the left wing, then going behind O2. Player O2 passes to O3 moving towards the middle court, then O2 goes behind O3. Player O3 passes to O1, and goes behind O1, who has moved toward the sidelines and back toward the middle. Player O1 passes to O2 for the lay-up shot. The player rebounding the ball dribbles back to midcourt along either sideline, while the other two players use the defense shuffle, with arms behind their backs, trying to keep pace with the dribbler. This gives two players the opportunity to practice the defensive slide skill.

The following shots can be attempted off the weave: (1) right or left-handed lay-ups, (2) the right- or left-handed power lay-ups, (3) the **baby** (short) jumper, and (4) the sky-shot.

Several plays to be practiced originate off the weave. The first one is the 1-on-1. Diagram 31-2 shows the three-man weave with this play. The play starts on the third pass. The receiving player yells, "Ball Game," then waits temporarily for the passer to guard him; they then play 1-on-1 for one basket or until the defensive man secures possession of the ball. The third player waits for the completion of the play, then the player with the ball dribbles back to midcourt and the other two players use a defensive shuffle as they move up the court. In the diagram, O3 is the passer making the third pass to receiver O1. They play a 1-on-1 and O1 yells, "Ball Game."

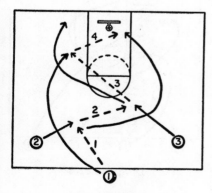

Diagram 31-1

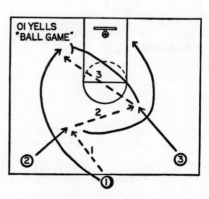

Diagram 31-2

The next play is the 2-on-1, shown in Diagram 31-3. The action in the diagram follows after the three-man weave has been executed. Player O1 hollers "Ball Game" and he and O2 play 2-on-1 against O3. Player O1 dribbles toward the basket and passes to O2 for the lay-up as displayed in the diagram.

The third play is called **Suicide,** and is the 1-on-2 (one player on offense, and two on defense). In this play, when a player receives the third pass and yells "Ball Game," the other two players attempt to prevent him from scoring. If the offensive player rebounds a made or missed shot, the two defensive players try to prevent the offensive player from scoring. This type of play continues until one player scores three baskets.

The next play is the 2-on-2. Screen-and-roll plays are practiced in this type of play. This play originates from the four-man weave. The weave leads to the 2-on-2 on the fifth pass. The passer guards the receiver, while the player further from the basket defenses the player closer to the basket. Diagram 31-4 shows the play starting with the four-man weave then leading into 2-on-2 play. Player O2 sets an inside-lateral-screen for ball handler O3 to begin play against O4 and O1 (now X4 and X1). The play ends after each basket, or possession by the defense.

The final play is shown in two parts. Note diagrams 31-5 and 31-6. It is a six-man weave followed by a 3-on-3 play that permits utilization of various screens and cuts. The six-man weave originates at the defensive baseline, using the entire court, thereby giving more opportunity to execute a successful six-player weave. To simplify this play the players choose teams prior to the start of the

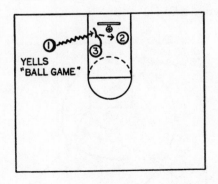

Diagram 31-3

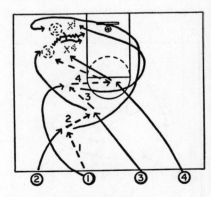

Diagram 31-4

drill. In Diagram 31-5, the weave takes place until O6 receives a pass at the free throw circle and yells "Ball Game." The players quickly set up to play 3-on-3.

Diagram 31-6 shows the 3-on-3 teams and a play. Player O6 with the ball, O1 and O2 are on offense playing against X5, X4, and X3. Player O6 passes to O1, who cuts off O2's outside-lateral-screen, then moves to the right-wing position for the shot. The play terminates after a score or a defensive rebound.

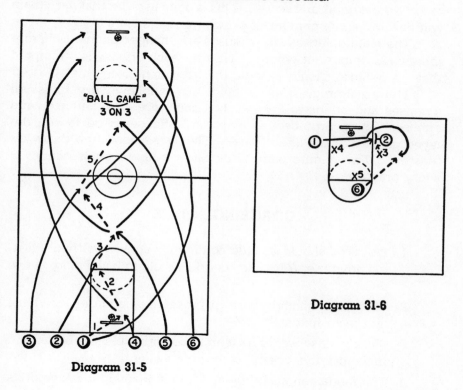

Diagram 31-5

Diagram 31-6

Multiple Control Scrimmage Drill

This drill makes is possible to review and practice the defense, transition, and the offensive systems. Both regular and substitute player development is a by-product of this drill, as both the first and second teams play an equal period of time in all phases of this drill (Tip 39).

The object of the drill is to permit one team (Team A) to begin with a full-court press, while the other (Team B) tries to use a press breaker offense, or an appropriate patterned offense to score. If the shot is successful, then the teams switch roles. If the shot is unsuccessful, the defensive team can rebound the ball and execute the Transition fast break, Phase-one, and Phase-two.

At this point after the made or missed shot, the ball is given to Team B on the appropriate end of the court, even if Team B has executed the break and scored. (This is done in order that each team will have an equal number of starting possessions.)

The team defenses and offenses are changed as the drill progresses. (An important point is that after each offense is attempted that the defense should execute the transition break.)

The usual progression of the drill is as follows: first, pressure defenses and offenses. Second, half-court pressure defenses and offenses. Third, drop-back defense and offenses. And fourth, delayed game defense and offenses. The Ten-second free throw offense and Two-minute game drill follow and are implemented in every practice.

COACHING POINTS

1. Practices should include continuous activity without wasting any time. A less active drill should follow a more active one.

2. The coach should insist on proper execution of individual and team fundamentals.

3. More intense workouts tend to condition players better and make playing a game somewhat easier.

4. The fundamentals in the multiple fundamental weave drills and the multiple control scrimmaged drill should be varied.

5. For variety, request that a different cut or screen play be executed during each possession drill, when practicing the 2-on-2 and 3-on-3 plays.

6. Interchange players often in the weave and control-scrimmage drills, so they become accustomed to each other.

7. Do not stop when a player is fouled in either drill. Make the player who fouls run laps, after the drill has been completed.

8. Both drills should end immediately when a violation occurs.

TIP 32

Use Qualitative Fundamentals Practice Games

OVERVIEW

There are two approaches in practicing fundamentals. One is the qualitative method and the other is the quantitative method. The qualitative method is using fundamentals in the exact same way they are executed in game competition. Quantitative method refers to practicing a fundamental out of game competition. The drill used does not actually fit into a game situation; instead it provides an opportunity for a player to become skilled by practicing a more isolated fundamental(s). Both methods are necessary because the quantitative method helps players learn the basic skill, while the qualitative method gives players the opportunities to use the learned skills under game conditions. We use qualitative fundamentals games drills to practice various special game situations.

The games are more enjoyable to play, in addition to helping the players learn the various fundamental skills and a variety of team maneuvers. There are six game drills we use that have been extremely helpful in teaching the players the various special game situations. They are (1) the **Pressing game,** (2) the **Fast break game,** (3) the **Two-minute game,** (4) the **Jump Ball Game,** (5) the **Out-of-bounds under-the-basket game,** and (6) the **Take-a-charge game.**

These games take up little practice time and are of great value considering the little time invested during the course of a season. It does not take much time to play a two-out-of-three game series or to play two or three different games in one practice session. This is especially true in the latter part of the season when it is necessary to add variety to maintain a high level of interest in practice.

183

EXECUTION

The rules of each game will be explained along with the point system utilized. You might want to use the first team against the second, or change player combinations from time to time.

The Pressing Game

This game is designed to be played while using all of the pressure defenses, pressure offenses, and the Transition fast-break phases one and two. There is a break in the action and ball possession changes after a basket has been scored, a violation, or when the offensive team completes the Transition phase two without scoring (Tip 10). Points can be made by either the offensive or defensive team. The object of the game is to score twenty-one points to win.

The **Pressing game** is played in the following manner. One team is given the ball out-of-bounds under their defensive basket and attempts to move the ball up-court and to score a basket. The other team uses one of the full-court presses designated by the team quarterback (assign a different quarterback each game) to stop the offensive thrust. Set up a Transition fast break seeking to score a basket within ten seconds after securing possession by rebounding a missed shot, intercepting a pass, or stealing the ball (maximum time to utilize the Transition game phase one and two). Play stops immediately after any violation or basket. The team that was initially playing defense then has a turn at passing the ball in from their defensive baseline and to attack the opponent's pressure defenses. Every time the game stops, the teams switch offensive-defensive assignments. In other words, if the first team throws the ball in and the second team intercepts the ball and scores within ten seconds, the second team gets its regular turn on the offensive, even though they scored. Points can be scored in the following manner:

1. One point for the offensive team if they penetrate to the free throw line extended.
2. Two points for a basket scored.
3. One point for every free throw made.

4. One point for the defensive team if they steal a ball or make an interception, or if a violation is made by an offensive player.

5. Two points for a basket made within ten seconds after ball possession on a steal, interception, or rebound by the defensive team.

A variation may be to put the ball in play along the sidelines in the backcourt. Another is to have the defensive players switch positions on occasions.

The Fast Break Game

This game is designed to utilize the Transition fast break phase one. Quick scoring plays within five seconds is the objective. The game is played in the following manner:

Play begins with a jump ball at center-court. The team possessing the ball is given five seconds to shoot. The other team can use only three players on defense until the first shot is attempted. A fourth player may assist his three teammates on an offensive rebound. The other team should fast break immediately after gaining possession or after a basket has been scored. However, the defensive team (permitted to have three defenders) can keep only one of the original three players on defense during two consecutive attempts. The other two players have to be two that were not on defense during the previous attempt. This game is continuous and the object is to make twelve baskets to win the game. (Players fouling must run laps after the game is terminated.)

The Two-minute Game

This game is designed to develop and practice late game strategy. Winning or losing the close games can make the difference between a winning or losing season. Players should learn how to win the many close games a team plays during the course of a season.

The game is played in the following manner (and always at the end of practice).

There are two minutes left in the game with the score tied and a jump ball at center court. Each team has a captain who designates the defense and offense for his team to implement. Both teams have one time out remaining. This type of game should be played with a clock and a referee. The team ahead when time has expired wins the game. In the case of a tie score, the first team to score two consecutive points is the winner. A variation is to set up any score situation desired. Also, playing a best of three game series can make the games very interesting.

The Jump Ball Game

This game is designed to help players react to jump ball situations at the various circles against players of different sizes and jumping abilities. Twenty points constitute a game. The game is played in the following manner:

A different player from each team jumps each time, with the jump ball situation originating in a different circle each time. The team winning the tap has ten seconds to execute a jump ball play, followed by the two phases of the Transition break, if needed.

Points may be scored in the following manner:

1. One point for possession of the tap.
2. Two points for making a basket.
3. One point for each free throw made.
4. One point for an interception, a steal, or a violation forced by the defensive team.

The Out-of-Bounds-Under-the-Basket-Game

The object of this game is to develop, practice, and refine both the offensive and defensive aspects of the under-the-basket situations when inbounding the ball. The game is played when a team takes the ball out of bounds, then tries to inbound the ball and score within ten seconds. The ball switches hands after each play attempt. Both teams must have equal chances to score. The team that scores 16 points wins. (In case both teams are tied, they play a sudden-death playoff.)

Points are scored in the following manner:

1. Two points for a basket made within ten seconds after inbounding the ball

2. One point for every free throw made

3. One point for blocking an inbound pass attempt (defense), even if the offensive team retains possession

4. One point for the defensive team if they intercept a pass or steal the ball

5. One point for the defensive team if a violation is made by an offensive player

6. One point if the offensive team retrieves an offensive rebound

Play stops after ten seconds and no shot or change of ball possession.

The Take-a-Charge Game

This game is designed to practice recognizing charge-taking situations, taking the charge (Tip 8), and avoiding the charge.

In this game, the offensive team starts with a player dribbling at midcourt. The team on defense can use any type of team defense. The offensive team uses the appropriate offensive pattern. The object is to have the defensive players set up offensive charge-taking situations. It takes twenty points to win the game. Points are scored in the following way:

1. Two points for making a basket.

2. One point for each free throw made.

3. One point for the defensive team making a steal, an interception, or a defensive team violation.

4. Two points for the defensive team when a player can take a charge successfully.

5. One point for causing a defensive blocking foul.

COACHING POINTS

1. Hold brief post-game discussions pointing out positive and negative plays.

2. Have losing teams run laps or line-touches.

3. Select a different player to repeat score, time left, and other points relating to the game situation, out loud, on game delays during the Two-minute game.

4. Assign a captain (quarterback) for each team to make play selections.

5. Use games more often late in the season.

6. Play the Two-minute game at the end of each practice.

7. The games should be competitive and enjoyable for the players.

8. Encourage players to offer creative ideas for establishing new plays.

TIP 33

A Comprehensive Pre-Game Day Practice

OVERVIEW

Although every practice is significant when preparing a team for a game, the pre-game day practice plays an important part in winning or losing. It is in this practice that the players and coaching staff should make final preparations physically, psychologically, and emotionally, to perform up to their highest level of ability.

All of the hard work in previous practices can be of little value if there is insufficient or too much practice, or if the wrong emphasis is made on the various aspects of the game. In short, the practice should be well-planned in content, emphasis, and length of time. Coaches have their own ideas about practice schedule as to the length of time that should be spent on the various aspects of basketball. Players are very adaptable; consequently, they will adjust to coaching methods and philosophy. The important point is for you to plan practices which are based on sound physiological and psychological principles.

After years of personal observation and some research, I discovered that well-planned, hard, short workouts are the most practical for pre-game day practice. This is especially true in the latter part of the season. Many teams leave their championships on the court in the pre-game day practice by overworking rather than easing up. Some evidence that over-practice is physiological and causes an anaerobic condition (fast movements creating oxygen debt), and an aerobic condition (slower constant movements with little oxygen debt). Players can become physically tired and will recuperate at a slower rate with **excessive practice** using either anaerobic or aerobic type drills. A slow recuperation period affects a player's game performance the following day.

189

EXECUTION

The pre-game day workout should not last longer than one and a half hours early in the year, and should be cut down to one hour and fifteen minutes during the last half of the season. The exception to this rule is holding a one and a half hour practice if it is the only session prior to the game. (For example, no practice on Sunday, practice on Monday, and game on Tuesday.) The players can tolerate and need a longer Monday workout because of the rest and the need to sharpen up team skills and to overcome the inactivity over the weekend or Sunday.

The pre-game day practice is similar to focusing the lens of a microscope. Every part of the team system, game plan, and psychological attitude should be in clear focus. Individual and team skills as well as team system of play should be fine tuned in this workout.

The sound pre-game day practice should be guided by the following five criteria:

1. Practice should be of a short duration.
2. Players should practice rather intensely.
3. All aspects of the game should be reviewed.
4. Shooting should be practiced with a purpose.
5. Practice should be fun.

The following pre-game day practice has worked out well for our teams. The individual fundamental will be listed and discussed. The length of practice time allotted for each will also be indicated.

Pre-game Day Practice Schedule and Fundamentals

1. Stretching Exercises—5 minutes; general upper and lower body stretching.

2. Weave-Multiple Drill—5 minutes (Tip 31). You can omit the four- and six-man weaves.

3. Two-man Team Shooting Contests—10 minutes; play around-the-world games with two-man teams. Each team competing against all the other teams.

4. Defense and Run—15 minutes; the first team practices the planned game defense against the second team. The first team transition fast-breaks (Phases One and Two) against only three defenders. Then the second team does the same at the other basket (both taking equal turns—see Tip 39).

5. Scrimmage Ten Points—10 minutes; a regular game with the first team playing against the second. The team scoring ten points wins. The purpose of this scrimmage is for the players to execute the offensive and defensive patterns properly. Offenses and defenses are designated for each team, by the coach.

6. Ten-Second Last-Shot Offense—8 minutes; after opponents shoot free throws (Tip 28), each team maintains ball possession unless lost by a violation, turnover, or defensive team rebound.

7. Pressure Free Throws—7 minutes; two players at a basket with one ball. Coach sets up hypothetical situation for example, "Two points down, shooting a one-and-one free throw." If either player misses, both players do five sit-ups.

8. Two-Minute Game (Tip 32)—10 minutes; team selected at random. (May play three game series, especially in early season.)

9. Team Twenty-Five Free Throws Drill—5 minutes; five players at each basket. A shooter with two players on each side of the lane in proper defensive free-throw alignment. The player shooting attempts two shots. If shot is successful, all players holler out the total baskets made, then rotate clockwise to a new position. The drill ends after twenty-five baskets are made. (Player on the lane, practice blocking out and rebounding the ball on every other shot.)

Formal practice ends with a players' huddle and the coach making the final comments.

The practice can be extended to one and one half hours at your discretion. You can elect to use the extra fifteen minutes in areas where the team will benefit most.

COACHING POINTS

1. An injured player expecting to play in the game should practice. He should work out lightly by stretching and shooting on his own, while observing the workout.

2. You should resist the temptation to extend the practice time.

3. There should not be any practice on game days unless a team is on an overnight trip. This practice should be held in the late morning. Limit should be to a half hour or less. Practice should consist of a warm up, shooting, and ending with a free throw tournament.

4. Vary the Weave-multiple drill, the shooting, and the free throw drills to maintain interest, but keep the others intact.

5. Simulate an opponent's basketball court if you are playing an away game and their court is unusual in some respects. For example, difference in the size of the court, distance of court from the stands or wall, and the lighting.

6. Strive to establish a confident, determined, and optimistic atmosphere in practice.

7. Make sure that the players attempt to execute offenses and defenses **properly** during the checkout, drills, and scrimmage.

8. Permit the captain(s) to direct the squad through some of the practice drills.

TIP 34

Techniques and Drills
For Improving
Free Throw Shooting

OVERVIEW

It is estimated that over 40 percent of the games can be won at the free throw line, according to a random sampling of game statistics. Probably more significant than that estimate is that a high percentage of games are kept close or are runaways because of made or missed free throw attempts.

Another important factor is that success or failure at the free throw line can influence team morale in a positive (if successful) or negative (if missed) manner. A final point is that made or missed, free throws can influence scoring momentum. The obvious conclusion then is for players to become outstanding free throw shooters.

In high school basketball a team average of 60 percent to 64 percent is good, 65 to 69 percent is considered very good, 70 to 74 percent is excellent, 75 to 79 percent is an outstanding average, and 80 percent or over is classified as superior. In college each category should be five percent higher in order to obtain the same ratings. Players' experience, strength, and poise is the reason for the difference.

There are many coaching theories on how to develop free throw shooters. These theories all center on the following areas: The important basics in free throw technique, psychological outlook, emotional control, concentration, and practice. Each of these areas will be discussed in addition to an explanation of several practice drills.

EXECUTION

The most common free throw shooting method is the one-hand set-shot. One reason for this is the close correlation between the jump shot and the set-shot. Another reason is that it is easier to teach this shot. Occasionally a player may learn to use the two-handed under-handed method (the highest percentage shot) or the jump shot, but both are rare exceptions rather than the rule. Therefore, the discussion will center on the one-hand set-shot.

One-Hand Set-Shot Technique

The underlying essential to this shot is the body balance. A player should have body balance prior to, during, and after releasing the ball. One foot (same foot as shooting hand) should be a few inches ahead of the other, and about shoulder width apart. The knees should be flexed slightly. The player should bend his back in the waist leaning forward. The ball should be held chest high in one hand, and in line with his shoulder on the side of his shooting hand. The shooting hand should be behind the ball, with the ball resting in the hand. The other hand should be on the side of the ball helping to balance the ball in the shooting hand. The shot should take place after a rhythmic smooth move generating from the feet and progressing up the body in a whip-like action, first with knees bending then straightening out. The elbow unhinges, extending the arm up as the wrist flapping action helps to propel the ball, as the player rises up on his toes and back down on his feet. Again the rhythm should be down, up and shoot with balance.

Psychological Outlook

A player should block out excessive thoughts when preparing to attempt the free throw shot. The main thoughts should center on the game situation and his defensive assignment; the player should eliminate negative thoughts and think of positive ones. For an example, he should see himself as an 80 percent free throw shooter. He should visualize the ball going through the basket. His attitude should be "you either do or you don't."

Emotional Control

Relaxation is the key to controlling emotions. You should understand that each player handles emotions differently. One player may relax by moving around excessively while another might need only to adjust his weight from one leg to the other. One player might want the full ten seconds allowed in a free throw situation, while another might want to shoot immediately upon receiving the ball, while another might prefer to bounce it on the floor several times. Each player should find the most suitable relaxation routine—deep breaths or tightening and relaxing muscles (particularly the shoulder, arms, and neck muscles)—and follow it consistently.

Concentration

A player should also learn about his concentration pattern. Too often coaches assume that a player should concentrate on the target or at a basket for a longer period of time than necessary. A player should experiment to find the optimum rhythm that will permit him to hit a "concentration peak," at the precise moment the shot is being attempted. The shooting rhythm of the various players will also tend to vary in length.

Practice

It takes practice to become an outstanding free throw shooter. There are not any short cuts or magical ways to learn. Many hours should be spent on all of the points mentioned. The free throw practice plan should be established for the entire season in order to develop each player. The plan should include shooting many free throws consecutively to develop technique, style, and rhythm, plus a limited number for concentration and statistical evaluation (charts should be kept in practice of each player's accuracy). Finally, pressure situation free throw shooting should be emphasized and included in the plan.

The following drills have proven successful throughout the years. They make it possible to develop the essential fundamentals necessary to develop outstanding free throwers.

1. **50-and-Go Drill.** This drill used in the pre-season at the end of practice. Each player shoots fifty shots before he can go to the showers.

2. **Percentage-Time Drill.** This drill takes place in early season during practice. The player shoots ten free throws (five at two different intervals) and the results are charted each day. His shooting percentage is established for the week and also is cumulative over several weeks or a season.

3. **Swish-or-Run Drill.** This drill is used during some practices. Each player shoots ten free throws. He must make a minimum of seven out of ten attempts without hitting the rim. Players failing to make the minimum run one line-touch agility drill.

4. **Special-Situation Drill.** This drill is used in various practice sessions throughout the season. The procedure is for the coach to stop practice at some moment and send two players to each basket. The coach gives various situations such as two points down, shooting 1-and-1. If a player misses the first free throw attempt, he should run two laps; if he misses the second, he should run one lap; if he makes both, he does not run any lap.

5. **Sudden-Death Tournament.** This drill is held at the end of practice. It is a two-shot, sudden-death elimination tournament with one winner. (In case of a tie between two teams, the tournament continues until one player makes a free throw and the opposing player misses.) The losers run the line-touch agility drill.

6. **Make-or-Break.** In this drill the coach stops regular practice momentarily, calls for a 1-and-1 free throw situation, then selects the shooter. If he shoots and misses the first attempt, the entire squad runs two laps; if the second one is missed, they run one lap; if both tries are successful, the players do not run any laps. (A variation of this drill is to have each player shoot and run if he misses.)

7. **Eight-in-a-Row Drill.** This drill is held at the end of some practice sessions. Each player has to make eight straight free throws before being dismissed from practice.

8. **Two-Man-Ten-in-Row Drill.** This drill is also held at the end of some practice periods. It is similar to the Eight-in-a-row drill except that there are two players on each team. Each player alternates by shooting two shots at a time when at the free throw line, with the object being to make ten consecutive free throws before being dismissed. (Players shooting the tenth attempt might be harassed by teammates.)

9. **Team Twenty-Five Drill.** This drill is used at the end of a practice period. Five players are at one basket with two on each side of the lane and one player shooting. Each player shoots two free throws each time he is at the line. Then the players rotate clockwise. The object is to make a total of twenty-five free throws.

10. **Longest Streak Drill.** This drill is held once a week near the end of practice. Each player shoots until he makes a free throw. Then he keeps count of how many shots he can make in succession. Each player records his longest consecutive streak.

COACHING POINTS

1. A player can develop form, rhythm, and muscle memory by shooting a great number of shots at one time.

2. A player should step back from the line if he misses the first of a two-shot free throw attempt.

3. Do not worry about missing a free throw. Concentrate on the free throw to follow or the ensuing action.

4. As the season progresses, free throw drills should be held at various times during the practice session—when players are fresh and at various stages of fatigue.

5. Keep the head still during the free throw shot.

6. Concentrate on the center of the rim as the target.

7. Establish a century club for free throwing (make 100 free throws without missing). This was Coach Virgil Sweet's idea at Valpraiso High School, Valpraiso, Indiana. He gave emblems to players who succeeded.

8. Award a trophy to the player with the highest free throw percentage at the end of the season. This should be based on a minimum of thirty-five free throws.

TIP 35

Develop Individual Player Toughness

OVERVIEW

Basketball players should learn to absorb body contact and some physical mistreatment during a game. There is a tremendous amount of contact that takes place in a game, and the player has little or no equipment for protection. Consequently, a player must learn to protect himself and permit the minimum amount of abuse in contact situations. This should be practiced to prevent a player from changing his style of play in excessive contact situations. The best conditioner for absorbing contact is to encourage basketball players to participate in the high school football program. Football is a sport predicated on players being knocked down and getting up again while absorbing physical abuse. This can be extremely beneficial for a basketball player as the player could be conditioned for diving on loose balls, rebounding, setting screens, taking the charge, and being bumped, pushed, held, or tripped during the regular process of play. For players lacking experience in football or any other contact sport, they can be toughened by using special drills that involve contact. The drills should generally be used early in the season. The toughness type of drills can be used for physical conditioning as well. By using a weight program for strength, contact drills for toughness and conditioning, the players should acquire and maintain a high level of strength and toughness.

College players who participated in high school football also reap the toughness benefits. They should retain the toughness throughout their college basketball careers. There is not any need for them to play football at the college level, although if the player wants to play, it could be quite beneficial. The big problems include the overlapping seasons as coaches insist on year-round concentration and practice in one sport, and the chance of injury. Usually by the time a player attends college, a player decides to put emphasis on one sport.

However, it is wise to include toughness drills in both the high school and college basketball programs to develop and maintain toughness in specific basketball type contact.

EXECUTION

The following category of toughness drills have been instrumental in helping our players. We call them the **Survival-18 drills**. Many are used early in the season while others are used continuously. The **Survival-18** can serve the purpose for any coach wishing to use them, with the highlight being the various forms of contact practiced in conjunction with skills performed in a basketball game. Following is an explanation of the **Survival-18** drills.

1. **Up and at Him.** All players line up in four lines. One player acts as a leader and faces the group. The players follow the leader, who runs in place then performs a stunt and bounces up to resume running in place. The leader may:

- Fall backward and bounce up
- Fall backward and roll once right or left, and bounce up
- Fall frontward and bounce up
- Fall frontward, roll over once, either right or left, then bounce up
- Fall backward, make a backward somersault, and bounce up
- Fall on his stomach, make a forward somersault, and bounce up

2. **Two Man Mirror.** Two players face each other. One player leads and the other player follows (mirrors) his actions. The leader can execute any stunt he wishes. This goes on for twenty to thirty seconds. Then the two players change roles. It is important to give each pair of players sufficient floor space to avoid contact with other players involved in the drill.

3. **Donahue's Dive.** This drill is named after Coach Glen Donahue, Head Mentor at Highland Park Community College, Highland Park, Michigan, who designed the drill. Glen's team even uses it in pre-game warm-ups. The players form four lines with one player as a leader facing the four lines. The leader signals verbally, "Ready, Dive," and the leader and each player dive forward as far as possible, contacting the floor first with their chest, with arms outstretched, and dive sliding several feet on the floor. The players then come to an upright position in another direction. This is continued until the players dive in four different directions. In the back dive the players dive and make a turn and in the same motion, maneuver to a prone position again.

4. **Bull in the Ring.** Several players get into one of the circles on the floor. On a signal, they try to bump each other out of the circle. The last one remaining in the ring is the winner. Players should learn to stay in a relatively low position with feet spread well apart. As a variation, players can hop on one foot instead of having both feet on the floor.

5. **Push Around.** Two players execute this drill with both players facing the basket immediately outside the three second lane. One player stands in a rebounding blockout-type position with the other standing behind him or her. The back player attempts to push the other towards the basket. The player being pushed resists by keeping his feet spread apart and his body in a position low-to-the-floor.

6. **Block Out Ball Bounce.** Note Diagram 35-1. Three offensive players are spread out in a triangle around the three second lane (O1 on the left side, O2 at the foul line, and O3 on the right side). The three defensive players guarding them, X2, X3, and X4, are positioned between O1, O2, and O3 and the basket. The coach, stationed at the top of the free throw circle, shoots the ball. The object is for the three defensive players to box out the three offensive players until the ball hits the floor and then gain possession. If the offensive players control the ball before or after it hits the floor, they receive a point. If it hits the floor first and the defensive players gain possession, it is a point for the defensive team. Four points constitute a game.

7. **Circle Block Out.** This drill is shown in Diagram 35-2, with three offensive players, O1, O2, and O3, standing outside and three defensive players, X2, X3, and X4, standing inside the free throw circle. A ball is placed in the middle. On a signal by the coach, the

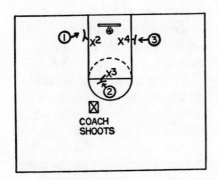

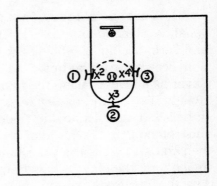

Diagram 35-1

Diagram 35-2

three defensive players try to black out their opponents, preventing them from gaining possession of the ball until the coach blows his whistle.

8. **Suicide.** This is a competitive rebounding and scoring drill. The coach shoots the ball and two players standing on either side of the basket try to secure the rebound. Immediately upon securing possession, the game begins. The first player to score three baskets is the winner. All shots are to be taken inside the lane. There should be a minimum of fouling in this drill.

9. **Bring the Ball Home.** This drill is played with the two players on each team standing outside the center jump circle facing a basket. The coach stands on the side of the circle. (See Diagram 35-3.) The coach rolls the ball into the circle. All players try to gain possession of the ball by diving for it. Immediately upon ball possession, the teams should play two-on-two full-court for one basket, by trying to score as quickly as possible. In the diagram, O1 gains ball possession then passes to teammate O2, breaking for his basket. This game may also be a one-on-one, or three-on-three type of contest.

10. **Bring the Ball Home Charge Drill.** Another version of the game may be played with two opposing players at the free throw circle. The coach should roll the ball into the circle. The player gaining possession should attempt to score with the defensive player taking a charge on the attempt.

11. **Get Up and Take the Charge.** This drill is shown in Diagram 35-4, with player X2 lying down near the free throw line and O1 with the ball at the top of the circle. On the coach's signal, O1 dribbles to the basket, and X2 tries to come to a standing position and take the charge.

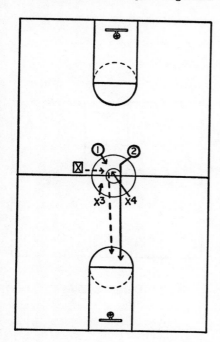

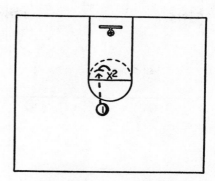

Diagram 35-4

Diagram 35-3

12. **Run Over.** This is a similar type drill with the one player lying on the floor near the free throw line and the remainder of the players lined up near the top of the circle. On a signal the players run and jump over the player lying on the floor. He may get up and take a charge from any teammate about to make contact with him. The player should lie down and repeat the drill again. The other players are spaced about ten feet apart. They reach the baseline then continue to run back near the top of the circle to secure a position in the line again.

13. **Payne Charge Drill.** This drill is another method to set up a charging situation. Coach Vern Payne, Head Basketball Coach at Western Michigan University, designed it to teach players to take a charge when a dribbler pivots to change direction (note Diagram 35-5). Dribbler O1 moves from the midcourt area to the twenty-eight foot hash mark, then makes a reverse spin dribble and heads towards the basket. Meanwhile, the defensive man X1 moves in position to take the charge.

14. **The Bump-Bump.** (Shown in Diagram 35-6.) Player O1 has the ball and is guarded by X2. Player O1 dribbles toward the free throw line. The coach yells "bump," and X1 moves in to bump a

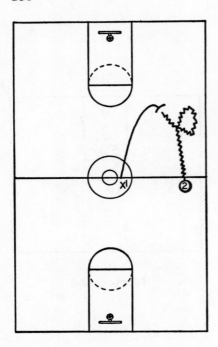

Diagram 35-5

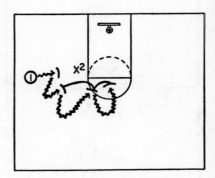

Diagram 35-6

cooperative O1 who bumps back. Player O1 continues dribbling, then backs up and begins moving forward again when the coach calls out the signal and the same bump-bump action is repeated. The drill ends on a signal given by the coach. Player X1 should bump O1 with his chest while O1 should use his shoulder opposite the ball.

15. **Lay-Up Rough-Up.** In this drill, the coach stands under the basket near a line ready to shoot lay-ups. As each player shoots, the coach makes contact by pushing, bumping, or grabbing the player. The players in the shooting line may dribble to shoot, or catch a pass to shoot.

16. **Screening Repeater.** This drill is shown in three diagrams (35-7, 35-8, and 35-9). It is designed to teach players to screen, to defense screens, and to avoid taking the full impact of the contact. In the first diagram (35-7), the coach has the ball at the top of the free throw circle. Four offensive players line up in a two-two stack on either side of the lane and are guarded man-to-man by the defensive players. The offensive players at the top of the stack execute down-screens to free teammates coming to the ball to receive a pass from the coach. If the coach passes the ball to a player, as in the

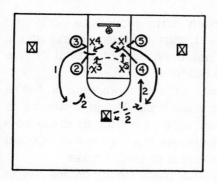

Diagram 35-7

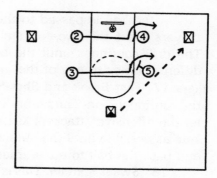

Diagram 35-8

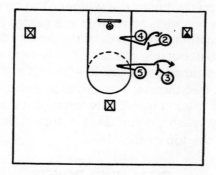

Diagram 35-9

diagram, the player immediately passes it back to the coach and the screening continues.

Continuing on with the drill, if the coach cannot pass to a player, the ball is passed to another coach on the wing side. The players quickly regroup to a two-two stack and begin outside lateral screening (players nearest the ball set the screens) trying to free a player to receive a pass. If this is not possible, then the players receiving screens return to set outside-lateral screens for their teammates. This action is depicted in two consecutive diagrams, 35-8 and 35-9. In Diagram 35-8, the coach has the ball on the right side. Players O4 and O5 set outside-lateral screens for O2 and O3, to come to the ball. Since neither has received a pass from the coach, they then go back to screen for O4 and O5, who faked cuts across the lane prior to accepting screens as they move toward the coach (note Diagram 35-9). A variation of the drill would be to permit players to change the type of screens set (for example, lateral-inside, up or down screens).

If the ball is passed to the coach at the top of the circle, the players reset the two-two stack and start down-screening again. The drill continues until the ball has been passed a total of five different times to any of the three coaches.

17. **Fast Break and Shot-Shot.** This is an innovation added to the continual 3-on-2 and 4-on-3 fast break drills. The innovation is to let the offensive attackers keep shooting and scoring as many baskets as possible until the defensive players can secure the rebound and pass the ball to a teammate to break to their basket.

18. **Sweet Sixteen.** This is a regular game played on one basket with five players. (The player possessing the ball plays against the other four.) Each player keeps his own score, with the first one scoring sixteen points being the winner. The coach starts the drill with a shot then proceeds to referee the game. Players may shoot from anywhere within fifteen feet of the basket. They cannot, however, move the ball outside the lane if it is retrieved inside. Otherwise, regular basketball rules are in effect. If a player is fouled, he should shoot the free throws. The bonus free throws rule is in effect at all times. On a missed free throw attempt the ball is in play; on a made free throw each player takes a turn gaining possession to inbound it from the top of the circle.

COACHING POINTS

1. Teach players to fall correctly to avoid injury.

2. Players should avoid taking the full impact of a bump by using their arms bent at the elbows and hands to ward off an opponent, or move with the bump.

3. Use a variety of drills to practice the various types of contact.

4. Players should develop mental toughness—overcoming the fear of getting hurt—with careful planning and use of toughness drills.

5. Players should be taught to use their arms and hands to protect themselves when taking a charge.

6. Players should learn to play rough but clean.

7. Players should learn to use peripheral vision to avoid oncoming contact.

8. Keep out of drills the injured players who are in a condition in which further injury could result from the contact.

TIP 36

Practice Jump Shots
Off Seven Moves

OVERVIEW

Approximately 60 percent of the shots in a basketball game are jump shots. Jump shots are attempted from within a few feet of the basket to beyond twenty-five feet.

There are various fakes and moves preceding a drive to the basket, often followed by fakes and moves at the completion of the drive and preceding the shot. An explosive start and a sudden stop are all methods by which a player can either move closer to the basket or give the offensive player some more room to shoot the jump shot, without having it blocked.

The term **pure jump shooter** can be misleading. It is a term referring to an outstanding shooter. However, outstanding shooters may not necessarily be outstanding scorers. In my perception of the term, a **pure jump shooter** must also be a good scorer. My definition then is **a shooter with an outstanding touch, capable of making a high percentage of shot attempts.** The greater the distance the lower the shooting percentage. These shots should take place after various types of fakes, moves, and drives. A great shooter should shoot and score rather consistently from a variety of maneuvers and in various situations.

Outstanding shooting tends to cover up for many mistakes in basketball. An offense pattern may be ill-timed or poorly executed, but successful shooting makes the offense look much better. Just the opposite is true with the missed shots that make a smoothly executed offensive pattern appear inadequate. Much has been written and discussed about the importance of defense and rebounding. As important as these two aspects of basketball are for winning games, shooting is probably more important than either of the other aspects.

A player can learn to be an outstanding shooter by practicing the proper technique, and by having a desire to score. Going one step further, the player should also learn to shoot the jump shot by using seven different moves. These moves are designed to encompass a variety of methods a player can utilize to get free to shoot the jumper, thereby creating more scoring opportunities.

EXECUTION

There should be a brief review of jump shooting techniques prior to the explanation of the various moves.

Jump Shooting Techniques

The jump shot has five basic fundamentals. The first is body balance. Footwork is important to establish and maintain body balance. The correct stance is to have both feet parallel or one foot slightly ahead of the other. The feet should be approximately eight to twelve inches apart in both methods. The body should maintain balance prior to, during and after the shot.

The second fundamental is to move the shooting arm elbow up, with the hand in a cocked position holding the ball in line with the shoulders. The ball should be resting near the finger tips of the shooting hand. The other hand should be on the side of the ball, to help to hold it in place. The non-shooting hand should not assist in propelling the ball. It is for the purpose of stabilizing the position of the ball until it is released. The front of the player's body should be facing the basket.

Jumping into the air and shooting the ball is the third fundamental. To jump, the player should bend his knees, then straighten them out, propelling him up and off the floor.

The ball should be shot by straightening out the elbow with an unhinging type of move, then releasing the ball with the arm and hand fully extended.

The fourth fundamental is for the player to concentrate on the target as the ball is being released. A player should concentrate and shoot for the center of the rim. The eyes should focus on the center of the rim until the ball goes through or hits the rim.

The fifth fundamental is the follow through with the arm extended at a high level, with the wrist folded over. The player should then land on the floor at the point of the takeoff. Only the legs, arms, and hands should move on the shot. The head and torso should not be used. One final important point is that the shooting process should follow a three count rhythm pattern:

1. **set** (catching and holding the ball and establishing balance position),
2. **aim** (ball in ready position immediately below the eyeline, concentrating on the target), and
3. **shoot** (shooting the ball).

Seven Different Moves

Before explaining the moves, it must be mentioned that a fake(s) may be made prior to a move or jump shot. Also, a forward or reverse pivot can be made prior to shots close to the basket, particularly by a post-man. The explanations will not include fakes.

The first move includes two types of pivots. The Forward-pivot-and-shoot move is displayed on the right side of Diagram 36-1. The forward-pivot move is shown from a low-post position with the player's back to the basket.

On the left side of Diagram 36-1 is the Reverse-pivot-and-shoot move. The player, with his back to the basket, drops his left foot back towards the basket, then makes a reverse pivot in order to face the basket and to shoot.

Diagram 36-2 shows move number two, the Drive and stop. Three different drives are shown from immediately outside the top of the free throw circle. Player O1 drives right, mid-way between

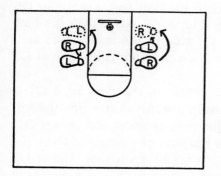

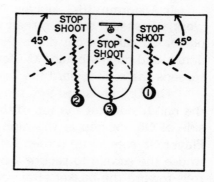

Diagram 36-1   **Diagram 36-2**

the baseline and the 45 degree line, stops, and shoots. Player O1 should use the backboard on this shot attempt. Player O3 drives directly towards the basket, stops, and shoots, while O2 drives to the baseline area, stops, and shoots (aim directly for the rim circle from this baseline angle). A move could also originate from the left or right wing positions with the player driving into the middle of the three-second zone.

Stopping is very important in getting free for the shot. The correct form is for the player to keep low when stopping. This permits the player to stop quickly because the center of gravity is lower and therefore the player can maintain better balance in preparation for the jump shot.

The third move can be initiated anywhere in the jump shooting area. It is the Fake-drive-and-shoot move. The player receives a pass, faces the basket, fakes a drive by taking one big step forward with his lead foot, then bringing the foot back under him to maintain balance and shoot with the body under control.

In the fourth move, the Give-go-and-stop, a perimeter player passes to a wing player, then cuts toward the basket to receive a return pass within fifteen feet of the basket. He stops and takes a jump shot.

Close-the-gap is the fifth move. This move is used whenever a player with the ball is guarded loosely. The player should execute this move by making one quick dribble, then release the ball from a knee high position, while taking two quick steps toward the basket. He then picks up the ball with both hands and shoots, before the defender can react to the move.

The next two plays (six and seven) involve shooting behind screens and are depicted in Diagrams 36-3 and 36-4.

In Diagram 36-3, player O1 with the ball and wing man O5 work a Pass-and-return screen play. Player O1 passes O5 the ball, player O1 fakes a cut down the right side of the lane, stops suddenly, and moves behind O5 for a return pass and shot. Player O5 screens the rolls toward the basket.

The Dribble-screen-go move is shown in Diagram 36-4. O1 is the ball handler at the top of the circle. He drives towards the left side of O5, located at the high right post position and facing O1. Player O5 sets an up-screen for the purpose of veering to the right to use the screen to secure a position for an open shot. Player O5 rolls toward the basket after screening to be ready for a pass or a rebound.

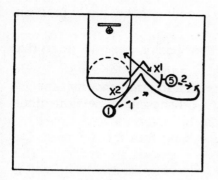

Diagram 36-3   **Diagram 36-4**

The Sam Washington Shooting Drill (Sam is Basketball Director at St. Cecilia Gym in Detroit, where outstanding players of all ages participate in games, and is also General Manager of the Detroit Spirits, of the Continental Basketball League) is good for conditioning, and for practicing various moves and jump shots. Here is how the drill works. Four players position in the two wing positions and two guard positions. They are twenty-three feet from the basket. They pass the ball around to each other and a fifth player (the shooter) follows the ball around until receiving a pass. Then the shooter makes a move towards the basket, stops and shoots a jump shot, retrieves the ball, then passes it to any of the other players. The same procedure is repeated until the shooter makes eight or ten baskets. Different moves should be tried each time.

COACHING POINTS

1. Players should learn to fake a shot and drive, then fake a drive and jump shoot.
2. Strength is important for long range shooting accuracy. Players should use weights in the off season to develop shoulder, arm, and hand strength.
3. Use fakes often when close to the basket, especially against an overanxious defender.
4. Help players master the quick stops that are so essential to getting free to shoot.
5. Good passers make good shooters. The shooter should be given the ball at the optimum time, thus permitting the shooter time to rhythmically "set, aim, and shoot."

6. Players should use the same shooting technique in practice as in a game.

7. Players should be aware of floor position in relation to the basket at all times.

8. A player can develop an outstanding jump shot by practicing on an outdoor court in the off season. During this time he should also be working on the seven moves.

TIP 37

Motivating Players With A Merit System

A coach's primary responsibility is to instill in players a desire to realize their fullest potential. Although physical ability is a key element in athletic performance, an equally necessary element is **motivation.** You should be aware of each player's capabilities, help him set goals, and encourage him to perform at his best. The difference between an average performance and a superior one is the incentives based on the different factors that drive a player, in addition to potential ability. The focus of this tip is to discuss player motivation, then to explain how to develop a practical merit system to motivate players. A sample merit system program has been outlined.

Motivation (making a person move toward an end based on needs, interests, and drives) is a major ingredient for success in athletics. Psychologists have developed psychometric techniques to evaluate the personality traits and motivational factors of athletes in general. The psychometric technique can help make you aware of each player's individual strengths and weaknesses.

You should also use a perceptual method to gain insight into a player's personality; this insight will be used in dealing with a player's motivation. Players can improve performance by having the coach observe their behavior and determining their needs.

Each player has his own motivational drives. A combination of incentives can motivate him to greater achievements. Personal recognition, ego-reinforcement, self-realization, fear, proof of masculinity, material gain, the need for an emotional outlet, the need for purely physical movement, and the need for physical fitness are among the most common sources for a basketball player.

If a basketball player is to realize his potential, he should possess a positive attitude. This can be developed through setting goals, through encouragement, desire, confidence, and determination, along with planning. The goals should be short, intermediate, as well as long term.

Techniques to be used to develop motivation by coaches are praise, threat of punishment, diversion from failure, gimmicks, use of voice, individual and team discussions, and pep talks.

An important aspect of athletic performance is tension. A certain degree of tension is necessary, but an extreme degree hinders achievement. You should be sensitive to differences in tension among your players, as each builds his own tension level. In determining the ideal level, you should rely on experience and apply the general rule that sports involving simple motor skills are performed better under greater stress, while complex motor skills are performed best with a lower degree of tension, since emphasis is placed on fine muscle coordination. (Basketball has both simple and complex skills, with the emphasis on the latter.)

The competitive nature of basketball provides the player with the opportunity to succeed and to realize his own potential. It also helps an individual to develop self-awareness and learn how he reacts to stress and challenging situations.

Practice sessions in basketball should be well planned, lively, and involve all members of the team. They should be both exciting and enjoyable. During practice, it is your responsibility to demand the excellence that is realized through discipline and player dedication to purpose. This is possible if you are concerned primarily with motivating players to perform to the best of their ability.

Extrinsic and Intrinsic Motivation

Motivation stems from both internal and external sources. When the origin of a drive is from within, is done for its own sake—it is intrinsically motivated. Performance in a skill or participation in a sport is for personal reasons, namely joy, satisfaction, or skill development. Intrinsic motivation implies ego involvement and self actualization (developing personal creativeness).

An extrinsically motivated person persists at an activity for the material gain received from it. Intensive effort is made not so much to enjoy the game, but to receive recognition, glory, and material gain instead of the comradeship, inner satisfaction, and achievement.

From an educational basketball program point of view, intrinsic motivation is more desirable than extrinsic motivation. It should be noted, however, that both intrinsic and extrinsic factors may operate concurrently. You should realize this when designing a program similar to the one to be discussed later.

It is the intrinsic reward that is important (like the cake itself). The extrinsic reward a player receives is like "frosting on the cake."

Achievement Motivation

The merit program should take into consideration the following principles in order to evolve around the basic premise that intrinsic motivation is the main ingredient even though extrinsic motivation is also used.

The need to be competent and to achieve underlies the potential for success. The players having a high need to achieve usually:

1. Demonstrate an extremely high persistence at pursuing and excelling in the game of basketball.
2. Demonstrate exceptional quality in performance.
3. Demonstrate complete skills development at a high level.
4. Are task oriented rather than person oriented.
5. Take reasonable risks and enjoy stress.
6. Like to take responsibility for action.
7. Like to have knowledge of the results of the performance (drill or game).

This player should be responsible for his own performance, rather than the coach. Personal decision-making and a perceived personal control over the situation should lead to a greater player commitment. This hopefully would be true once an understanding has been reached regarding the value of the program.

Planning the Merit Program

The coach and players should plan a merit program together. The program might be modified from season to season if both agree to make changes. The main principles of the program should include:

1. Discussion between coach and players about the purposes of the program.

2. Working together, the players and coach should set specific, high, but obtainable goals under the coach's guidance. Goals should be short term, intermediate, as well as long term.

3. Procedures to achieve the merits should be explored.

4. Once the program has been determined, personal records should be maintained. They can be used primarily for self-comparison but can also include comparison with others.

5. Wherever possible, feelings of self-confidence and self-image should be enhanced. Positive reinforcement by the coach is helpful.

6. There should be a constant reevaluation of the progress and the achievement rate of the player.

Tentative Merit System Program

The program about to be outlined is a very functional and one that takes into consideration the principles of a program. It is based on a "star" type program as used in football for a number of years. Every time a player achieves one of the specific goals, he would receive a star (or any other insignia—such as a basketball decal, for example). The stars might be different colors to signify the category of the achievement. (Green for academics is an example; red for defense is another example.)

The stars might be posted on a master bulletin board in the locker room, or on a player's personal locker.

. Here are some suggested ways a player might receive a star:

1. Academics:
   a. If a player attains a certain G.P.A. that was set by the coach and the player. The G.P.A. should be the present, past, and overall, such as a 2.5 or better.
   b. Perfect attendance in classes for a semester; or for the year.
2. Conditioning preseason:
   a. specific timing for a one mile run.
   b. specific timing for a two mile run.
   c. maintains established weight level.
   d. follows prescribed weight training program.

3. Practice:
   a. perfect attendance.
   b. excellent execution of drills.
   c. designs a drill which can be used during practice sessions.
   d. running the agility line touch drill under 20 seconds.
4. Game:
   a. holds a scorer to 50 percent of his average (if the team uses a man-to-man defense).
   b. takes three charges in one game.
   c. makes three ball recoveries or steals in a game.
   d. passes off five assists in a game.
   e. secures ten rebounds in a game.
   f. blocks three shots without fouling in a game.
   g. 60 percent shooting for a game (minimum of six shots).
   h. accumulates fifteen straight free throws in consecutive games.
   i. if team holds opponent to 60 percent of its scoring average (and wins the game).
   j. any other outstanding feat in a game as judged by players and the coaching staff.
   k. selected as team player of week for effort and hustle.

Evaluate the players each week for play progress during the season. Finally, the player receiving the most stars, when the season has been completed, should receive recognition in the form of a trophy for his consistent and outstanding performance.

TIP 38

Overcoming the "Choke-up" Syndrome

The most damaging criticism made concerning an athlete is to label him as a **choke-up.** His physical performance can be assessed as poor, which can be disturbing, but it is devastating for the press, the coach, the fans, or the players to imply that he chokes in critical situations, or bluntly stated, he is a **choke-up.** This inference often can permanently damage an athlete's ability to perform as well as affect his development in all phases of the game.

Choke-up, by my definition, means the inability of a player to perform the necessary skills in relation to his capability in a crucial situation and is caused by the emotional state of the individual. The **choke-up** title apparently was derived from a description of the physical feelings of tightening of the muscles in the neck. This feeling is prevalent when a person becomes tense. The throat becomes dry, and breathing, along with the heart beat rate, accelerates. These are normal feelings for any player in a critical game situation. Some players perform well at this time while others have definite problems.

CAUSES OF POOR PERFORMANCE

What causes players to perform at levels beneath their physical capabilities in certain situations? Most psychologists associate **choking-up** with the fear of failure. Failing means criticism and/or lack of acceptance by others, which is a basic need in life.

Basketball is a game which demands that players be aroused. Arousal means extremely active functions by the body systems,

219

particularly the nervous system. It is a game of individual player action, such as running, rebounding, shooting, and passing, to name a few. It is a game of team action with players maneuvering offensively within a pattern with the ball or off the ball. Yet, probably the most critical situation in any team sport is also part of basketball; that being the free throw. Action is stopped while the unmolested player is given an opportunity to shoot the free throw. The attention of everyone in the arena is focused on the shooter as he attempts the shot. It is strictly up to the player at the free throw line to succeed (make the shot), or fail (miss the attempt). It is obvious then that the players must be able to control their emotions in order to perform up to expectations in all aspects of the game, and particularly at the free throw line.

Many players are given the title **the Choke-up** permanently. The feeling is that they cannot overcome this habit of poor performance at critical times.

Players can overcome the **Choke-up** syndrome, and I will disclose the method by which it can be accomplished. First, it is necessary to find the causes and then analyze an individual to determine why his emotions overcome him to the point of having physical failure. In order to do this, it is important to study emotional behavior. For a starter let's look at a description of emotions, stress, and anxiety.

Emotions

The word emotions means **agitation of feelings** (from the French word **emovoir**, which means to stir up). Emotions may be referred to in two ways:

1. As a conscious experience of feeling.
2. By the psychological changes that take place within the body as a result of it.

Emotions are physiological and psychological responses and reactions resulting from perceived situations. There is not any doubt then that emotions, much like motivation,' may have an organizing or disorganizing affect on performance. Maturation brings about the development of many emotions, although many can be learned and conditioned.

Stress

Stress is the state that disrupts the homeostasis (internal body equilibrium) of the body. Any situation or activity can be perceived to be stressful by anyone at any time. The greater degree of perceived stress, the stronger the reaction to it. Stress is usually manifested in a heightened arousal state. The affects of stress are desirable at some times and undesirable at others.

Some basketball players perform better in practice than in a game, while others perform better in a game with an audience. Still others perform quite similarly in practice as in the game. It is also true that some players perform better than others in some stressful situations. This is particularly true for players lacking experience in a situation. It is obvious then that proper practice and experience in a situation helps a player perform closer to expectations. The transfer of skill efficiency in this case, from practice to a game, is positive and desirable. Two final points are:

1. Stress is usually more disruptive for the learning and performing of complex tasks than simple tasks.
2. If the skill has been learned well enough, the effects of stress will hardly be noticeable. In many cases, stress will improve performance with increased practice.

It is interesting to note that stress may or may not have a disruptive influence on an individual depending on the player, the situation, the stage of skill ability, and the surrounding conditions. Understanding the emotional nature of each player will make it possible for you to help the player to a greater degree to overcome these emotional problems.

Anxiety

Anxiety is the tendency to perceive a situation as threatening or stressful. Anxious feelings as a reaction to stress are commonplace. An important factor for coaches to understand is that anxiety can be viewed as two distinct concepts instead of one. **State anxiety** refers to how a person feels at a particular moment in response to a specific situation and is a transitory emotional state. **Trait anxiety** is the general disposition of individuals to respond to psychological stress and is relatively stable. Particular events can bring out different emotions from the same person; also some players have more consistent behavior patterns than others. The highly skilled player learns to adjust to emotions appropriate to the demands of the activity. Too much anxiety will hinder the performance of any player.

An important point in analyzing a player's emotional performance is that the source of the problem can fall into two categories:

1. When anxiety is due to the situation, more experiences with the situation should be provided for in practice time.
2. When anxiety is due to the person, relaxation techniques should be learned.

Where anxiety levels are well beyond desirable range, a particular relaxation program might be helpful.

Relaxation Programs

In recent years, there has been an emphasis on our fast paced American society to find ways to relax the body and the mind. There have been many programs designed to serve this purpose. Basketball coaches have turned to some of these methods to help their players reduce anxiety and tension in practices and in games. There is some evidence that these relaxation programs have been helpful to some players, but they are not a panacea for all. Because the programs for relaxation may be helpful, it is worth naming and describing some of the more popular ones.

In **biofeedback training,** the player learns to identify indicants of his personal emotional state through the use of feedback information from various devices. The devices measure brain waves, pulse rate, muscle tension, galvanic skill response, temperature, and emotional response. Training should help a player quiet his internal state.

In **meditation programs,** the idea is to free one's mind of stress by concentrating thought and feeling of inner space. Concentration may be on a particular word or image. A state of complete relaxation and increased energies to undertake impending tasks are the goal.

In **anxiety reduction programs,** people learn to relax muscle groups. Afterward, the learners internally identify situations that normally arouse anxiety in them and attempt to produce relaxation in those situations. Irrational anxiety is thereby decreased.

In **progressive relaxation programs,** a particular muscle group is tensed deliberately, then relaxed. This relaxes the muscles to the point at which they can function better.

Methods of Overcoming the Choke-up Syndrome

Now that the in-depth study of performance, emotions, stress, anxiety, and relaxation programs has been made, the next discussion is a plan to overcome the syndrome. The review would serve as the basis for each method mentioned. The necessary ingredients evolve around player's attitude, skill preparation and ability, and emotional relaxation and control. All team members can benefit from these methods; however, in some cases you may also desire to work more intensely with one or more individuals. The key issue is that a team will play many close games and players will be involved in many critical situations during the season. You should know each player's performance capabilities and seek ways to help each player perform to the level of his potential. Understanding each player's personality should help you to understand the player better.

The suggested coaching methods are as follows:

1. Help players develop the following attitudes:
   a. Seek to perform at their optimum level.
   b. Be willing to take a chance without the fear of failure.
   c. Accept the fact that there are times when you will fail.
   d. Keep a game in proper perspective; a win or loss is not as important as it might appear initially.
   e. In a critical situation, execute fundamental skills properly, and attempt to follow the game plan.
   f. Do not dwell on the past; emphasize what should be done in the future.
   g. **Expect** to succeed—not hope to succeed.
   h. Play intelligently.
   i. Be patient.
   j. Winning and losing should be a team effort and responsibility.
   k. Develop the desire to have the opportunity to attempt a key play (meaning you want to be where the action is found).

    l. Encourage teammates.

2. Coaches should help players with skill development.
   a. Identify weaknesses in their game and practice overcoming these weaknesses.
   b. Practice the skill as it should be executed in game competition.
   c. Attempt to develop a 90 percent free throw shooting ability.
   d. Learn skills correctly.
   e. Attempt to develop a 50 percent perimeter shooting ability, and 100 percent on lay-ups.

3. Use situation practices—set up:
   a. Qualitative practice games (Tip 32).
   b. Practice free throw situations (Tip 34).
   c. Last second scoring plays (Tip 27). Alternate the players taking the last shot.
   d. Practice the Ten-second offense (Tip 28). Alternate the players in various positions.

4. Relaxation. Have players:
   a. Practice a relaxation program to improve relaxation.
   b. Use a ritual for free throws. Stretch muscles, bounce ball, deep breathe, and other methods that might assist one in developing a better free throw shooting percentage.
   c. Develop relaxation technique during game delays. Such as jump ball plays, free throws, and out-of-bounds plays.
   d. Develop relaxation techniques for use during time outs.
   e. Concentrate on the game process and the game plan.
   f. Work off frustrations by playing harder during all phases of the game.

Individual Counseling

Finally, one-on-one counseling sessions with players can be desirable if you understand a counseling technique. The player can often find it comforting to know that you are willing to listen, understand, encourage, and help that player gain personal insight when he is not performing up to expectation. It will be easier for a player to perform closer to his optimum ability if he gains insight into his own behavior and outlook on competition.

TIP 39

Developing a Ten Man Team

Championships are won by teams that have a good bench strength—five or more players who, in addition to the five starters, will see considerable action as dependable replacements at any time in a game. I have always advocated playing at least ten players (sometimes twelve) in each game. The players on the team are selected to play basketball, consequently they should be active basketball players. If the players are not going to participate in the game, then they should practice bench sitting skills, like how to sit, how to cross their legs, how to fold their arms, and how to turn their heads to follow the play. Naturally, these comments are ridiculous, but not any more so than using six or seven players throughout the season when there are always players sitting the bench worthy of playing and have the ability to contribute to each game.

The system of substituting freely has been successful for our teams on both the high school and the college levels. I realize that the style of play may influence the number of substitutions. A team pressing and running will need to substitute more than a team playing the "Rocking Chair" slow type of basketball. Regardless, there is a need to utilize substitutes for various reasons in both systems of play.

Championship teams generally emphasize the fast tempo game. They use full court defensive pressure, fast breaks, and considerable movement in their offensive patterns with shots developing rather quickly. The slowdown teams will inevitably end up as the losing team.

There are many coaches who claim the players on the bench have very limited ability and would hurt the team badly if called on to play. This is not necessarily true. Players often develop from substitutes to regulars when given an opportunity to play.

A coach should build bench strength by developing the substitutes. This can only happen when the coach takes sufficient time to work with the substitutes before and after regular practice and permits them to participate in games regularly. There is a big difference in development of players playing regularly and those making rare appearances in games.

The following is a list of fifteen reasons why the coach should develop a ten man team:

1. To give the regulars a chance to rest.

2. To tire the opponents. Ten players against six or eight should be an advantage, especially if both teams are equal in ability.

3. To be able to make changes if a player or players are having a bad game.

4. To replace an injured player(s) without weakening the team.

5. To prevent regular players from suffering burnout in the latter part of the season.

6. To prevent players from suffering tournament fatigue when called upon to play two or more games in a short period of time.

7. To keep substitutes game-sharp. Some players play limited or not any time for most of the season then are not able to perform well when permitted to play (rust-out syndrome). They cannot play effectively unless given an opportunity on a regular basis.

8. Players gain confidence by playing—lose confidence if they do not play.

9. Player morale is higher if more players are offered the opportunity to play.

10. A player might become a standout if given the opportunity to play.

11. The regular players work harder to improve when substitutes are fighting for their positions.

12. Young players acquire much needed game experience for the following year. (Avoiding an occasional inexperienced team.)

13. A player can go all out instead of pacing himself, knowing that a substitute will give him a rest period.

14. A substitute might have a hot shooting hand.

15. The coach can select various situation teams (more about this later).

For more information on how to develop a ten man team, see the techniques and methods to develop players discussed in Tips 31 and 32. Reference to utilize ten players equally in drills, scrimmages, and plays is made throughout the book.

Substitution Ideas

1. It is important that all players participate in the first half of the game. It is unfair to expect a player to come off the bench cold in the second half or the last few minutes of a pressure-packed situation and to perform at maximum capacity. Consequently, every player should see some action relatively early in the game.

2. Any time a ball player is fatigued and displays signs of not being able to maintain the game tempo, he should be replaced with a substitute, even if it means replacing an outstanding player. A tired excellent player is only mediocre, whereas a mediocre, rested hustling player might be excellent.

3. A coach should try not to substitute more than two players each time. Allow one minute for these two to warm up before sending in more players. (You can make an exception later in the game after all the players have played considerably.)

4. A player entering the game for the first time should race up and down the court with emphasis on defense and rebounding along with offensive pattern playmaking rather than on attempting to shoot immediately. The player should not force a shot, but allow the natural sequence of play avail him of shooting chances, waiting until he warms up physically and adjusts to the flow of the game.

5. A player on the bench should concentrate on the game progress at all times, looking to gain an insight concerning the opponents. He should actually feel as though he is playing. This will help the player to blend into the action somewhat earlier and with greater ease.

6. The substitutes should be permitted to play for several minutes rather than have to leave the game immediately, as short time periods really do not offer a player the chance to perform up to his potential capacity.

7. Starters in the second half should be players who have been in the game who have a hot-scoring hand, were rebounding well, or who have generally contributed to successful team play.

8. Play the second half with the players executing at top efficiency. Substitute for players with excessive fouls, those playing erratically, or who appear to be fatigued.

9. Switch the starting line up from time to time to experiment with different player combinations.

10. When substituting, use the following method:

a. Permit the starting team to play for a quarter, substitute two players at the quarter, two players one minute later, and the last substitute one minute after that.

b. Substitute earlier if a player collects two fouls, if a player is having a bad night, or if a player is loafing defensively.

c. Keep a player having a hot-scoring hand in until he tires or cools off.

d. Reinstall the regulars in the game with the 2-2-1 system mentioned above the last one and a half minutes to play in the half. This avoids keeping them out the entire second quarter throughout the half-time break. If the starters do not finish the second quarter, then the starter(s) should have a more strenuous warm up prior to beginning the second half.

e. Make appropriate substitutions when the second string is having problems on offense or defense.

f. Play the second half according to game progress mentioned above except, rest any tired players the first part of the last period, especially players who the coach plans to use the latter part of the game. This is especially true during a close game.

Situation Teams

A team for all occasions is another big plus emanating from a ten- or twelve-man squad. One can gain a great deal of satisfaction from developing situation teams for various purposes. There are many situations which call for using one or two players to gain an advantage (usually temporarily). Sending in an outstanding jumper or big man to control the tip on the jump ball at the beginning of each quarter; utilizing three different players to tire an outstanding ball handler; replacing a small point player with a taller player to take an opposing small player with a taller player to take an opposing small player into the pivot if the opponent is using the man-for-man defense are three typical examples. However, one can go a step further by inserting a complete team (an exception to the rule of not replacing five players at one time) for a specific purpose and on a temporary basis. Following are five teams and the purpose of each:

1. **The Rebels** is a team made up of five of the substitutes (including the eleventh and twelfth players sent into the game for a brief time period—two to four minutes) used to shake up the opponent, or to create turmoil in the game when your regulars are playing below their potential. The Rebels arouse the fans with hustling aggressive play while disturbing the opponent's game tempo and flow.

2. **The Pressing Demons** is a team composed of the five best pressing defensive players. Usually it includes four speedy, aggressive, alert, good shooting players with the best versatile big man. The purpose is to gain the lead back when losing by eight or more points at any time, but especially late in the game. (On occasions this team may be used to put a game out of the opponent's reach.)

3. **The Power Men** combination of players includes the four biggest, strongest rebounders with the best point man. The purpose is to use a tight zone defense against a big, tall opponents who do not necessarily shoot well from the outside preferring instead to play the inside game with strong rebounding. This power team can alternate with the Pressing Demons to keep changing from power to speed and finesse.

4. **The Precisionists** are made up of the five most capable offensive pattern execution players, regardless of player size (although at least one tall player is desirable for rebounding purposes). The purpose here is to keep executing the offensive tactics against the opponent's defenses with precision until finally setting up a shooter near the basket, with the other players in good rebounding and defensive positions. This team should work the best against excellent defensive teams who play fast breaking basketball, and are threatening to put the game out of reach.

5. **Tempo Controllers** are made up of three or four guards with the one or two best big players. These players should be the best ball handlers, and excellent free throwers. The purpose of this team is to use the delay game offense, shooting only lay-up shots and free throws. Its mission is to preserve the lead late in the first half or at the end of the game. The Tempo Controllers may also be used as a two-tempo team to utilize this attack throughout against outstanding opponents. The team should press defensively, fast break (the fast tempo) and hold the ball for a good shot using the opponent's scoring time (slow tempo). This two-tempo game works extremely well when the score is tied or when leading the opponent.

TIP 40

Utilizing a Computer to Evaluate Game Performance

This is the day of the computer. This wonderful machine is a big part of our life since it touches practically every aspect of our everyday living. Currently the computer is used by professional football, basketball, baseball, golf, and other sports for scouting, to compile, sort out, and display individual and/or team statistics, and for individual and/or team evaluation and tendencies.

A computer can be extremely helpful by serving similar purposes in your program. A wealth of interesting helpful information can be collected for you.

Most high schools have computer programming classes as part of the academic curriculum. Students have access to a computer in computer science classes. It is not unusual for a student to work on special assignments as part of the class assignments. It would be ideal for a coach to utilize the service of one of the computer science students. (Computer science classes and services are plentiful in a university setting, too.)

There are also inexpensive computers available which can be purchased by the athletic department. Some of these sets even have the printout accessory. There are training classes for those interested in learning how to use a computer. The BASIC language used is relatively easy to comprehend. There are also programmed tapes available for immediate use.

There are seven advantages for using a computer in a program. They are:

1. The speed and the volume of work. There is not any comparison in the speed and volume of work that can be produced by a computer compared to manual methods.

231

2. Accuracy—the computer is accurate. Humans make the errors, not the computer.

3. Variable results—this term refers to inputting a given amount of material into the computer. The computer turns out a greater amount of material involving different and varied analysis rather than only one set of information. The information turned out would include an analysis of a problem for an example, from several different perspectives.

4. Referrals—instant, general, and isolated information can be quickly presented either on the terminal screen or the printout, simply by pressing the correct key codes.

5. Storage—a great deal of information can be stored in the computer memory bank. The information takes little space and can be recalled in a short period of time. This makes it possible to add current information to older information to give cumulative totals, interpretations, or results.

6. Statistical analysis—the computer can be programmed to equate any mathematical formula necessary to figure out, to process, or to mathematically evaluate a problem. Any form of statistical analysis is possible.

7. A printout—the computer can display information on the terminal screen or on a paper printout. The paper printouts can be inserted in a loose-leaf notebook for future reference.

How a Computer Works

Here is a brief overview of how the computer works. The first step is to make a project plan. The plan should include all details of information to be measured or processed. The second is to make a worksheet for collecting data. After the data are collected, it should be fed into the computer by the punch card method or by typing the information into a terminal.

At this point, the computer is guided by the program developed for the project. The program indicates to the computer what should be done with the data. The program obviously is the key to using the computer. It often takes time to develop a program properly, but once completed it is good indefinitely. It can even be updated, modified, or changed to add or delete information whenever desired. (A wealth of material can be collected and processed from only one program.) The final step is for the information to be displayed on screen or in printout form, for analysis, evaluation, and planning.

Shot Attempts Analysis

Recently I designed a five part chart to gain deeper insight into the various types of shots taken and the play that was used to create the shot opportunity. The data collected made it possible to learn about the play tendencies a team may use to create shots as well as the type of shots, by using this chart over a number of games. The chart to collect the data is prepared by human beings, but the computer processes the data. The program for this chart is being prepared. My plan for this chart is to use it for the purpose of studying the actions and shots by teams on the high school and college levels.

The chart is depicted in five diagrams, 40-1 through 40-5. Each should be explained in the proper sequence in order for the reader to gain a more thorough understanding. The first diagram, 40-1, is an information page containing general information on players' names, height, weight, and other relevant information.

Diagram 40-2 contains the charting symbols. The object here is to substitute two-, three-, or four-letter symbols for the complete word(s). (This simplifies the charting while cutting down on the number of words, saving both time and space.)

The floor area is divided and is identified by letters A-H in the next part on the chart. (See Diagram 40-3.) Only the frontcourt from the four foot line to the basket is needed, as most of the shots are attempted by players in this area.

The Worksheet Information Chart, Diagram 40-4, includes the definition of the headings on the worksheet depicted in Diagram 40-5. The action of each play and shot is recorded on this sheet. It is from this worksheet that the information is taken and fed into the computer. It is important that each line include only one play. This type of design is ideal for computer work, because of the chronological order of gathering information.

INFORMATION SHEET

Team _____ Opponent _____ Date _____

Name	Position	Height	Weight	Number	Year

Diagram 40-1

CHARTING SYMBOLS

Type of Play

Screen	SC
Drive	DR
Baseline Drive	BDR
Pick and Roll	PR
One on One	O-O
Open Cut	OCU

Type of Shot

Jump Shot	JS
Jump Shot Dribble	JSD
Spin Jump Shot	SJS
Shot Made	
Lay-Up Shot	
Right	LUR
Left	LUL
Angle Right	LUAR
Angle Left	LUAL
Reverse Right	LURR
Reverse Left	LURL
Set Shot	SS
Hook Shot	
Right	HSR
Left	HSL
Flip Shot	
Right	FSR
Left	FSL
Tip Shot	
Right	TSR
Left	TSL

Diagram 40-2

FLOOR AREA

A   E
B   F
C   G
D   H

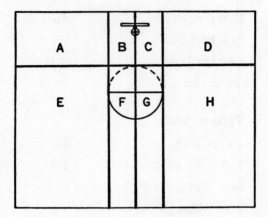

Diagram 40-3

WORKSHEET INFORMATION CHART
(May chart one or both teams)

Team Number Possessions (Refers to Team possessing ball.)

Home Team	1
Visiting Team	2

Player Number	Identifies the player
Type of Play	Action identifies the play
Type of Shot	Shot identified
Time	Time remaining in the quarter or the half
Score	Score when shot was attempted
Court Area	Area where shot was attempted
Comments	Any general comment for clarity

Diagram 40-4

SITUATION CHART

Quarter _____

Team Number (Possession)	Player Number	Type of Play	Type of Shot	Time		Score		Court Area (A-H)	Comments
				Min.	Sec.	Home	Visit		

Diagram 40-5

Variable Results

Earlier I mentioned variable results as an advantage when using a computer. It is important to give more detailed information concerning the meaning of this term.

The worksheet mentioned above has eight categories of information to record. The information can be processed in several different ways, thus making it more thorough, by using the computer. The first analysis would be to focus on the player. Each player would have his cumulative totals for the game and season.

The second analysis would focus on the type of play with the totals for the various plays summarized for the game and season. A third analysis would evolve around a format regarding the type of shot, while the court area could be a fourth analysis. The point I am making is that the variable analysis includes a different approach for emphasis and all of this is taken from one set of data collected. In fact, each category could be the analysis focus. Finally, a summary could also include a comparison of statistics between two opponents.

Game Analysis Chart

Some time ago, Coach Bill Sudeck of Case Western Reserve College in Cleveland, Ohio, along with the cooperation of Steve Spewek, a computer science major, developed a chart to determine many standard and unusual variables of a basketball game normally not charted, but in his opinion important to the outcome of the game. Included in the variables are shooting, rebounding, scoring, defensive errors, rebounding by positioning, and successful baseline drives, to name a few. The charting results were fed into a computer shortly after the game. (This process takes approximately one hour.) But the printouts with a wealth of information were completed by the computer in a matter of minutes. It is probably one of the best designed game evaluation computer programs in basketball today.

INDEX